# THE EDUCATION OF
# MR. WHIPPOORWILL

ALSO BY DAVID DALE ZIEROTH

BOOKS
*Clearing: Poems from a Journey* (1973)
*Mid-River* (1981)
*When the Stones Fly Up* (1985)
*The Weight of My Raggedy Skin* (1991)
*How I Joined Humanity at Last* (1998)
*Crows Do Not Have Retirement* (2001)

CHAPBOOKS
*The Tangled Bed* (2000)
*Palominos and Other Poems* (2000)

# THE EDUCATION OF
# MR. WHIPPOORWILL

## *A Country Boyhood*

DAVID ZIEROTH

Macfarlane Walter & Ross
Toronto

Macfarlane Walter & Ross
*An Affiliate of McClelland & Stewart Ltd.*
37A Hazelton Avenue
Toronto, Canada M5R 2E3
www.mwandr.com

**National Library of Canada Cataloguing in Publication Data**

Zieroth, David
The education of Mr. Whippoorwill : a country boyhood

ISBN 1-55199-097-0

I. Title.

PS8599.I47E3 2002     C813'.54     C2002-901061-6
PR9199.3.Z53E3 2002

Published simultaneously in the United States of America by
Macfarlane Walter & Ross,
P.O. Box 1030, Plattsburgh, New York 12901

Library of Congress Number: 2002105885

Macfarlane Walter & Ross gratefully acknowledges support for its publishing program from the Canada Council for the Arts, the Ontario Arts Council, and the Government of Canada through the Book Publishing Industry Development Program.

Printed and bound in Canada

This book is printed on acid-free paper that is
100% ancient forest friendly (100% post-consumer recycled).

For my two brothers and my sister,
in memory of our parents.

You are there in my memory, and in almost every man I
see; even men younger than I are somehow you –

– Russell Thornton, "Psalm"

## ACKNOWLEDGMENTS

I wish to thank Douglas College in New Westminster, British Columbia, for the educational leave that provided the time this book required. Thanks also to Robert Adams, Walter Isaac, Richard Lemm, Susan McCaslin, Calvin Wharton, and Mary Burns for their support, and to Judy Ferguson and Lucia Fuentes for the specialized information they provided. Thanks to Bernie, Arnie, and Vic for helping me remember. Special thanks for the editorial work and insights of Russell Thornton, Holley Rubinsky, and above all Gary Ross.

# — THE FARM —

The pregnant cow is chained to her manger. I'm in the section of the barn belonging to the horses, and from this safe distance – I'm behind a rough wooden partition – I watch while my father helps the calf arrive. He unchains the cow and then reaches into her rear. The urgency in his face tells me this is a critical time, not one to make myself known, though I'm sure he's seen and chosen to ignore me rather than shoo me away.

He tugs, and the calf comes tumbling out, a wet sack, slimy and steaming. The cow wheels around, the sack still hanging from her, and bends to her offspring. The calf stands, heaving itself unsteadily up, half staggering towards the underside of its mother. I'm aware of a new smell in the air – something of blood – that meets the other, older odours of hay and horsehair and animal sweat.

Dad wipes his arms clean on a grain bag. All seems well again. He gathers up the afterbirth on a pitchfork and heaves it out the back door. Then he leaves; but I stay, enthralled, watching from my perch, then climbing down to get closer to the calf. The mother is wary and she makes clear by the look in her eye and the low, angled position of her head that I would be wise not to touch her baby.

Then I notice a hoof sticking out of her, the top of her tail rubbing back and forth across it. I run across the yard to the tractor shed where Dad's working, fearful and thrilled to bear this news. He looks up from the forge where he's heating a tool. He puts down his hammer, says nothing while I awkwardly blurt out about the hoof, and starts for the barn before I've finished. Are we too late?

Again he pulls, and again a calf falls. This one doesn't struggle up on long, wobbly legs. It doesn't do anything. Dad scrapes the mucus from its nose, thumps and shakes the calf on the floor of the stable. The cow swings her head past it once, the briefest of investigations, then returns to the living one. Great scrapings of her tongue clean and sculpt its hair, dark, rich waves that will stay until the calf is washed in its first spring rain.

My father grabs the dead calf by the hind legs, drags it out the back door, and throws it onto the manure pile, head down. It'll stay there until the next time he hauls the manure away, to the west field – not long enough for the dogs to find it, although the magpies will soon arrive.

We name the living calf Moolee. She's weaned a few weeks later. We milk all the freshened cows, carry the milk to the house to be separated from the cream, then haul the milk back for the calves. They, of course, want nothing to do with it. We offer not a warm flank but a cold stainless steel pail full of skim milk.

Calves can suckle, but must be taught to drink. Some catch on easily, once they get hungry enough. They know the white stuff is milk; they try eating it, snorting bubbles in it, coughing in it. Dad pushes Moolee's head into the pail I'm holding until I think she will drown. He puts his fingers in her mouth; she gets a little milk by sucking on them. Mostly she wants to bump the pail, the way she bumped against her mother. I lose my patience and pull the pail away. She looks up at me, her big pink tongue sticking out. She seems stupid, a slow learner. Dad laughs when I yell at her.

Soon Moolee produces tiny bumps on her head, precursors to the horns that will grow and curve, shine and menace. We shave away the hair and smear on dehorning paste. "Now don't let her rub this off," my dad says. After a few minutes the paste begins to work: it burns down into the skin and kills the embryo horn. The calf's first reaction is always the same: she wants to scratch the itch caused by the burning ointment. She tries to reach it with her hind legs, tries pushing against the manger, finally tries rubbing against me.

It's my job to stand guard for three hours. This is my first experience of time's sloth; I'm required to be present but only in a minimally conscious way. I'm at the bottom of the pecking order again: my brothers aren't expected to do this. They've been assigned to cultivating, harrowing, or stooking. I spend the first hour trying to determine how I can tie up the calf so she can't touch her head. The last hour I sleep, falling into the sweet hay where the cats have found the sun.

Occasionally a calf grows up with horns. Daisy has only one, and it has had enough of the world that it's trying to grow back into her head, curling around and burrowing into her ear. Dad ignores it for a long time, but when there isn't room enough between the horn and the head to slip a dime through, it's time for the shears. They're a pair of pliers with sharp curved blades and wooden handles longer than my arms.

Dad chains Daisy to the manger. He slips the blades around the horn, slides his hands up the handles, then presses them together, his muscles working under his rolled-up shirt. Daisy bellows and turns her head as if to get away from the pain, but she's held by the blades – then the wrinkled, curved piece of horn pops away and blood runs down her white face. Dad smears ointment on the stump and leaves the barn, shears balanced on his shoulder. I follow, glancing back to see the cow watching us with bovine complacency. It puzzles me that, bloodied, physically harmed, she could be so utterly without malice.

❖

I'm often puzzled, though not yet troubled by my ignorance, as I see that beyond my knowledge lurks another world. My family makes no effort to conceal life from me, but neither do they seek to improve my understanding. It's only when Moolee comes into heat that I begin to wonder what's going on.

A bull is not to be trusted, my father says. After we milk the cows in the evening and turn them out to the corral behind the barn, he leads the bull out to drink from the trough. He clips a braided rope into the ring in the bull's nose. My dad knows a rope around the neck is folly; only the sharp jerk on the sensitive nose commands attention. The bull's neck builds into a great rippling hump atop his front legs; his curly, indented forehead covers a span of two hands. His horns curve, it seems, towards me. His hooves have curled under from too much standing around in the barn all winter. The large eyes glint of the madness of boredom. And hanging there, curiously, considering all that strength, the exposed scrotum, that pendulous sack the colour of sliced bologna.

I want to make him comfortable while he waits for his drink of water. I'd place a stack of newspapers under his wide head, and wouldn't he prefer the section that includes the comics? Vividly coloured lightheartedness to balance that massive, lolling strength. If I were the bull, I'd love the *scrich-scrich* of the funnies under my head as I settled in for the night's sleep, soothing me in my heavy power.

I'm just closing the corral gate when the bull comes thundering around the corner of the barn. Stretched out with speed, he shakes the ground. I don't know what to do. I'm surprised that Dad has let him out on his own.

I'm still trying to loop the wire over the gate but I know I'll never succeed. The fence is as high as I am. The bull weighs close to a ton. I watch in amazement as he leaps into the air and flies over the fence, landing in an explosion of dust in the corral.

At once the bull circles Moolee. He smells her rear and then stretches his nose in the air. His penis emerges from its sheath, a long red pointed crayon that bobs and dips. More circling, more sniffing, then the bull raises himself onto Moolee's back. I worry about the weight she must be bearing. The penis probes and then disappears. One thrust, and with the second thrust the bull's hind legs leave the ground entirely, his full weight driving Moolee forward. Like getting a needle, I think, a polio shot at school: some organizing beforehand – the lineup, the nurse rubbing alcohol on your arm – then the jab, the pressure of the stuff going in, the needle pulling out and the nurse moving on to the next pale kid. And something left behind: whatever was in the needle, now in me.

I've seen barn cats fighting, the roosters mounting hens before and after they strut, heard the squeals from the pig barn when the neighbour brings over his boar. When other farmers come to help with fall threshing, I hear new words. Some of the men speak with gestures as well. I'm in the loft of the barn, out of sight, listening, when I hear someone say, "You'd like to nail her," and then laughter.

When my dad comes up behind me to lead the bull back to the barn, we look at each other. I have a question, and he has an answer, but we can't put the two of them together. He steps through the fence, returning to his animals, and I wander off in the other direction.

❖

I love my father, and he loves me. This is the groundwork on which every presumption, every unspoken exchange, every nuanced expectation is built. He shows me how to handle a machine, or we bend our heads together over a tool, and he talks to me, and sometimes we laugh about something I don't understand. He tells me what to do, and I do it. I'm eager to help because I believe it will gain entry to my father.

My mother, on the other hand, is easy to talk to, easy to understand, easy to harangue and nag when I don't like the chores assigned me, the endless tasks no one else has time for. I can sit with her and shell peas into big bowls, or comb her hair into extravagant forms, making her ridiculous or pretty. I tie up her hair in poufs at the top of her head, and she laughs when she looks in her hand mirror. She doesn't mind this attention, nor does she mind sticking with me when I'm sick, gagging into the sink in the middle of the night because a big clot of blood has formed in my mouth where the extracted tooth was, her arms around my waist, leaning against my bent back and half gagging with me.

I can tell that my father is looking at me from the distance of the forty-five years he's already put under his belt when I'm born, the last of his four kids. He looks at me, then pulls away as if to reserve some strength for himself or for the others. After lunch, before he goes back out to his work, he lies on the couch in the living room to snooze for fifteen minutes, not really sleeping, eyes closed, doing some private calculation that restores him. Soon he's up and out the door with not much talking on the way. Perhaps he thinks I should've been a girl, devoted to my mother. I know from family legend that they were hoping for a girl, to bracket the oldest sibling – my sister – around the two boys born before me. The symmetry would have been pleasing, and perhaps my mother would have felt gratified, less cranky about the weight of work the farm puts on her.

Is it that my dad has taught the other boys everything he has time and inclination for, that to start up again would be too much effort? Of course, it's not work like cutting trees and throwing hay bales, but sometimes there's a weariness in his eye that says to me he's slipped away. I would like to follow him into his dreams, to see him the way he sees himself. Since I can't, I stay close to him, go where he goes.

He's taken the top off the barn well, ripping up its rotting wood floor. I come as near as I dare. "You get away from there," he says. I know, however, that I must look down the well. He's revealed a mystery, and I'm sure even he doesn't believe I should be denied the thrill of peering into its depths. I've often stood on this well and pumped water for the cows into the trough, thinking all the while of the descent into the dark if the floor were to collapse. I creep closer, and my father loosely grabs the back of my shirt.

Now I'm lying on my stomach, my father irritated but acquiescent. The pump itself has been pulled out and lies on the ground nearby, so I have a clear look down. The water twenty feet below flashes up its message, light caught down in the earth. I feel vaguely sick from vertigo, dizzy and intrigued, some part of me wanting to plunge in headfirst. The water – not as good as the water from the house well but good enough for the animals – smells strong and is brown from the presence of minerals, I've been told. I imagine it's tinted by the pee of the animals themselves.

I remember stories of children who fall in wells, understand there's no hope for the child who goes in. Were I to plunge down the slimy walls and break through the deep mirror, would I find myself on the other side of the world, living in a new family? Who would they be? How could I be sure they would love me?

I realize, startled, that even my father couldn't save me if I were to stand and stumble forward, into the well, all the way down. He realizes it, too. He tightens his grip on my shirt; he pulls me back.

❖

To milk the cows we must get them in the barn and tie them up. There seems no way to teach them their respective places except through routine. Each stall holds two cows, and each cow is chained. The older cows know what to do. The new ones – those who were free before giving birth to their first calves – are nervous and high-spirited.

We herd a new cow into her stall, but when Dad flips the chain around her neck, she panics and rears, her eyes big as cupcakes. Dad murmurs to her. I stand by the door with a pitchfork. She rips the chain out of the manger and heads for me. The other cows moo and stomp as I turn her back. Dad hammers a new board on top of the manger, secures the wild-eyed animal, then begins to milk her.

He strokes her flank and udder and then slowly and firmly begins squeezing her teats. She kicks; he backs quickly away. Her teats are small and hard to grip; he uses the two-finger method, like trying to milk a radish. He crouches and leans onto the cow, anticipating the swift and painful kick. He's very patient. I watch how he works. When I'm older, I will go from cow to cow with my stool and pail.

I'll tie up the tail of each cow, so she won't smack the side of my head when she's aiming to knock away the flies and mosquitoes that plague her. The older cows, with their tubular teats and big udders, will be grateful for the relief of milking. I'll rub salve on the teats that are chapped. I'll talk cow talk, to announce my coming near and my going away. I'll talk the way my father talks to the rough young cow, so she'll let down her milk.

When Dad is done, we check the cows' backs. He has shown me where warble flies lay their eggs at the base of the cow's hooves; when the eggs hatch, the larvae burrow under the hide and work their way up to the muscles of the spine, where they burst through the skin and hatch into flies again. Sometimes a hole the size of a small stone is left. Dad treats the cows with purple goo, not always successfully. He finds a warble larva ready to hatch, squeezes out the grub, crushes it under his heel. He rubs ointment into the hole to keep the sore from becoming inflamed and attracting magpies, who would like nothing better than to stand on the cow's back and peck out the soft flesh beneath the skin.

He checks for other things as well: for Bang's disease, which would mean the vet would have to come and vaccinate the herd. And pink eye, which the White Cow is prone to, her eye swelling up, multicoloured and watery, unseeing, in need of treatment. After the first dose, which Dad administers, it's my job to throw the pink dust in her eye for a week, to nurse it back to its painless shape and size. "It won't hurt her," he says, but I'm not so sure. Every morning and evening, as I'm about to dash powder in her eye, I smell its acidic, pungent odour, and I cringe. But the eye improves.

One morning we discover one of the calves will not get up, he's so bloated. Somehow he found a way to open the granary door – or perhaps someone left it open – and he ate more grain than he could digest. The seeds ferment in his stomach, turn into a mash of gases and juices that plugs him. He expands and grows, his organs pushing out his sides.

Dad finds a large whisky bottle made of heavy blue glass. He gets some Tide and pumps water into the bottle. He shakes the mixture and drops to his knees, raises the calf's head, and forces the remedy down its throat. The calf gags and chokes, but the detergent sets off a reaction and the troubled stomach soon throws up muck in a rush of putrid gas.

For the next three days, as the weather hangs in the high 90s, I splash in the tub by the house well. The cows push and shove to get at the water trough by the barn, and the Black Cow, the head cow, asserts her rights. In the evening, dark clouds climb out of the northwest. I know my dad is hoping the clouds will not bring hail; I've seen the places north of us where hailstones have stripped mature trees on one side of the road, leaving the other side untouched.

Late in the night the storm arrives. The clouds move in, and I'm awakened in my bed to hear my mother rushing through the house, prepared to hold pillows up against the big windows. I'm just about to pick up my own pillow when a lightning strike knocks me to the floor. I squeak with fear. Then the downpour begins, and my mum and I lean out the door and feel the black driving drops on our hands. We slide bowls out to catch the soft water.

In the morning we find one corner of the barn's roof torn off and the lightning rod charred black and bent. In the lean-to directly below we discover Moolee's calf, cold and blue and burnt around the jaw. I imagine the lightning travelling down the rod, then jumping from the loose, ungrounded wire through the calf's skull and into the earth below. I touch the calf's head and remember the bang of the lightning, a white fork dropping out of the night sky and searing down through the smooth, wet nose.

For my dad this death is a novelty, a story he tells in town on Saturday night at the Glen Café. Some men joke about roast beef, but most stir their coffees and cut their apple pie wordlessly, unable to laugh at loss. An animal killed in this way is worthless; there is nothing to be done with the carcass but to haul it out to the mound of stones in the west pasture and leave it for the coyotes. In winter I'll hear them at night; their wild cackling will push me down under my blankets as they cross the hard crust of snow, leaving no tracks, calling to my father, wanting to be fed by the farmer again.

❖

One morning my mother comments on my squinting, and by my first day in Grade 1, eyeglasses have become a part of me, often tilted on my nose and smeared with face grease or fingerprints. A six-year-old can hardly be expected to pay close attention to his appearance, especially the part he seldom sees. His glasses are like his mind: essential but not immediately noticeable from the inside.

By the end of the day I've met my first challenge: Ricky. The pretext of the fight is my glasses – how sissy they make me look – but the real issue is deeper, weirder, as if hard-wired into us. We flare and shove. I plan to counter his comments by rearranging his hair, but he's resistant. When I reach for his mop, he blocks my hand

and whips the glasses off my face. Then we're tangling on the ground, rolling over and twisting the glasses into a new shape. The bigger kids pull us apart. The lady teacher comes down from her perch on the high steps of the one-room school. Neither of us cries, because we know we simply cannot.

I'm thinking what my parents will say to me, the first child in the family to wear glasses. Will they have to drive the two hours to Gladstone again and talk to Mr. Finkleman, the optometrist, about their son the fighter? Will Mr. Finkleman look down and make me squirm in his leather seat, the lenses clicking and matching his own clicking disgust with boys who can't control themselves? I'm afraid this tall, severe man in his woollen suit and dark tie will be enraged by what I've done to his frames. Even my parents won't stand close to him, my father with the precious dollars in his wallet, his own glasses shining in the room's dim light, their wire arms curving behind ears that solemnly take in Mr. Finkleman's half-strangled utterances about the fragility of spectacles and the priceless nature of the eye.

Not long after my glasses are repaired, the bell cow loses her bell. It's my job to find it. I have to scour a half-section of bush pasture looking for something the colour of a stone, maybe under a bush, maybe in the dugout. I follow the main cow paths, trying to be methodical and optimistic. I hope to find the bell hanging on the fence. I work hard at looking, but I'm distracted by the cedar waxwings. I've found their nest high in the twisted poplar.

I walk past them deeper into the bush, less familiar with this area: the poplars grow like weeds here, higher than near the gate, and it's easy to lose direction. I keep an eye on the sun and remember which way I walk out of each clearing. I don't get lost but I don't find the bell either. It takes me all afternoon to give up the search. By then I've crossed the bush twice, ending each time in the low, muddy corner where the hooves of the cows leave half-cups in the ground. Here I'm far from home, and across the fence is land that belongs to a neighbour and looks foreign, although the poplars and willows seem identical.

Dad doesn't ask if I've found the bell. It's his turn now, and I watch him stride down the lane and into the bush. I play by the sandy part of the road, making trails and using little blocks of wood for trucks and tractors. I make the noises of machines and begin to get hungry. Then I hear the cow bell tinkling far off.

Dad comes out of the bush, not triumphant as I would have been. His cap's pushed back on his head. The breeze reaches the sweatband.

"Where was it?" I ask, squinting up at him.

"Just past the gate," he says, and mentions the clearing near the cedar waxwings' nest.

I return to my trucks and tractors and wonder how he's able to find what I can't, what special skill his glasses impart that mine don't give me.

❧

I cannot resist the swallows' nests. Dozens of them are wedged together under the eaves of the barn, high above me, each one a pouch made of mud and bits of hair and straw. Each nest has an entrance like a big teapot spout through which the adults enter and leave, tucking their wings at the last moment or clinging to the outside of the nest before darting inside. Occasionally nests fall, maybe too dry, no longer able to stick. These shatter into small chunks. Examining the bits, I discover the outer, rough, pebbled side, as if made up of spitballs, and an inner, smooth part. These opposites fascinate me, make me think: male-female.

Wings bear me from barn to house to yard pole, the morning cool on my feathered breast. I snap up mosquitoes with a flick of one wing and the wide-open cavern of my beak. I fly to school, stay outside, and listen to the teacher and see the other kids in tattered clothes looking out with longing, drawn by the breeze and by my abrupt, elegant twists in the wind. I call the kids out – those who can see me – and, to the surprise of the teacher, lead them into the sky. I tell them that never again do we have to stay inside on a sunny day. When we want to rest, we line up on the hydro wires, at first a dozen of us and then more and more until we're a dark line of shiny blue-black feathers. One by one we leap off and fly, higher and higher until we are specks above the burning green and golden fields.

But here on the ground summer days are long, and sometimes my hands are itching for occupation. I haven't been in school for weeks, and I want something I can do on my own without my friends. September is not of interest to me, too far in the future to cast its allure on these hot days.

To inspect the swallows' nests will require a ladder long enough to reach the eaves. I know my dad's ladder is too short; but he does fork hay up into the loft from the hayrack, and if I place the ladder on the floor of the rack, as I've seen him do, I might be able to reach. No, I'm not strong enough to drag the rack over to the barn, and I'm not sure of the steadiness of the ladder. Besides, it's too time-consuming.

The answer lies at my feet. Without thinking, I reach for a stone, aim, and throw it up. It plonks off the wall without hitting its target. I learn a great deal from that throw: I will probably hit closer to the nests by standing directly beneath the overhang and throwing the stone crisply underhand. It will go up like a rocket, if I'm lucky. It will break through the nest, and the nest will come tumbling down. If I'm really lucky, the stone will hit the edge of the roof, loosen a nest and send it whole into my hands. I'm ready to catch and inspect what falls my way, hoping fervently for eggs. I want to see their exact shape and colour, to feel their lightness. I'll prick a tiny hole in each end with a needle and blow out the egg itself. I'll keep the unbroken shell forever.

The stone strikes the cluster of nests, which explode into grey mud and dust. Pieces fall faster than I expect. Everything hits the ground before I can really open my hands. Two nests have come down, and with them two nestlings, ugly and naked, pink, mostly beak and feet, eyeless, bat-like with bony parts.

If my father comes around the corner of the barn now, he'll be angry. He's told me that the swallows are friends of the farmer because they eat the mosquitoes that torment his animals; they're life, and they're not to be treated without reverence. I feel my heart race ahead into consequences.

What would my father do now? I can barely imagine. He would never find himself in my place. I feel far away, as if he has abandoned me or died, though it's I who have left him, of course, disobeying what I know to be his first commandment: thou shalt not be stupid. I look down at the baby birds, their legs moving slightly. Are they near death from the fall? I must put them out of their misery. But how?

I take two boards that have blown off the barn and lay one in the muck. I put the babies on that board, place the other board on top, and jump on the top board, once, twice. I peel the boards apart. The two nestlings have become one smear.

My experiment complete, I throw the boards into the corral where the cows will chew them. The bits of nest I tramp into the muck so that no evidence remains of what I've done. My hands are innocent of real violence – not so my feet, which carry me quickly away but are not entirely successful in leaving events behind, holding me to the ground all through the summer so that thoughts of flying come less frequently and then not at all.

Guilt creeps into my face, I can feel it, and I work at appearing natural when I talk to my father, who has a superior ear for deceit in the most harmless of my words. I need to keep him away from my secret. He doesn't need to know how bad things can be.

❖

We have a few books in our house – some from church, some from school – and newspapers such as *The Western Producer, The Plumas Standard, The Family Herald*. My mother has a small inspirational book with a colour reproduction of a painting on the front cover showing Jesus praying in Gethsemane. She keeps it near at hand wherever she sits – by the heat vent; by the sewing machine covered by a white doily when not in use, the purple of the prayer book making the white shine; and on the small bedside table made by my father one winter.

My father's mother's three-inch-thick Bible, an illustrated German Bible, is one of the few belongings we receive from her generation. It's packed away by the time I arrive at my first great reading age, surfacing later in one of my sister's trunks. There I catch the packed-air aroma of old photograph albums, their pages of thick black paper. I see people who once stood shoulder to shoulder with my parents and whom no one remembers clearly any more, peering with their black and white faces into the camera.

Before we're introduced to the university's books-by-mail program, we are carvers and whittlers, knitters, inventors, putterers, nappers. I take a piece of cardboard, for example, preferably one from a good shoebox, not corrugated, and carefully stitch with my mother's crochet thread a flower with diamond-shaped petals. Or I erect a shape from my Meccano set and try to find the right adventures to populate these rigid little green girders.

My father spends his evening hours sifting through jigsaw puzzle pieces on the table, looking for just the right tone of blue sky. Sometimes I play cards with my brother, but often this results in too much noise: I am a poor loser, and I throw the cards in his face. He laughs at me, which makes me madder. Sometimes my father has to say a word.

When the first books arrive, we become unglued and drift into corners to savour them, our imaginations already firing, first at the smell, then at the individual marks – signs of former readers in the stains, thumb-prints, rips, underlinings, bent corners – and then, finally, at the stories they hold. My mother doesn't read these books, only my father and brother and me. I wonder if she *can* read. I know she went only to Grade 2, walking to school in her bare feet sometimes. I wonder how much there is she'll never know.

Sometimes the books we ask for are not available, and substitutes arrive. The librarian gauges who we are by what we order, hopeful that the unrequested titles fall within our range of interests. We can order only ten books at a time, and since the books come only once a month, we hope each will live up to the dream its title has inspired. I push my glasses up the bridge of my nose, and begin.

In one batch of books, deep in winter, I discover *Wild Animals I Have Known* by Ernest Thompson Seton. I read these stories before my dad; it's the largest book in the package, and the tales of wild animals shock and thrill me. Here is death: Lobo the wolf dies, the Pacing Mustang dies; all their mortal suffering touches me. I learn early on in these pages to look forward to the death. It's better to be prepared. Some survive – Silverspot the crow, Raggylug the rabbit – but the deaths of the others stir me, and I gorge myself on the sweet melancholy at the end of these stories.

The black and white drawings on almost every page show me some of the creatures I know from bush and field – deer, rabbits, partridges, dogs, crows. When I open the book, I'm entering familiar territory. And yet the book is not familiar at all: it reveals a secret. Here I'm told of the animal's life from birth, through the peculiarities of the time when it ran or flew full of blood and energy, to (often and best) its inevitable death. Outside, I only glimpse these stories.

I imagine that I'll meet a special crow with one white feather in its wing, a bird never seen on earth. It stays through the winter, living on the scraps a woman throws out her door every morning. Her husband doesn't like the crow, especially when the woman starts giving it more than fat trimmings, tossing it raw meat, bits she could use in their soup. But the woman feels no harm can come from feeding the poor bird through the coldest days. She imagines that this crow is not just a crow, that it has a power she's only beginning to intuit, and that if she can only find the right moment and the right words, she might be able to transform it into its true nature.

Her husband doesn't know about these wishes; he's been toughened by a life with animals – breeding, feeding, slaughtering – unable now to believe in anything other than their physical natures. Is the woman so unhappy that she will take flight with the crow one day, leave her body behind and rise up over the white fields, one loud *rhack* erupting from her mouth? I don't like the idea of her abandoning the husband even though he hasn't been understanding. I see how some part of the man's life has brutalized and limited his imagination.

I can't think how the story will end, so I replay my favourite scenes, especially the moment in the morning when the woman opens her door and tosses out pink scraps for the crow. (Are there no dogs to fight over these tidbits?) I see her looking up as the crow flies away, her husband in the house, scowling, unable to believe his wife can be so preoccupied by a bird. I don't know the outcome, can never imagine a satisfactory ending. Some change must take hold, but I cannot think whose force will prevail.

My father also reads the Seton stories and feels, I think, a vicarious thrill in the connection to other beings, a connection different from the working bond between farmer and animal. He looks bemused sometimes reading the book, his head tipped back a little to get the right distance for his glasses, his face younger than usual. Of the dog that is "a faithful sheep-dog by day and a bloodthirsty, treacherous monster by night," he says softly, "This is just the way it might be," speaking as much to himself as to me, pleased that the stories take him out of daily life and into a world familiar yet transformed, like a fairy tale. His use of the word "might" I begin to understand: it's a doubting word. But it's also a word that opens, that says the conditional can lead to confirmation and truth and thus stillness and peace. He reads, I see, not merely for consolation but for change.

*The Rise and Fall of the Third Reich* appears next in his hands; for many nights he's engrossed, and I see the white swastika on the black cover, the way it blocks out his face, its shape so insistent that it seems only now has its movement been arrested, as if it has flown onto the cover where it sticks. I see that my dad is enjoying and being swallowed by this book. He's close to the pages, furrowed and riveted, his face not younger but enthralled, not wanting to capitulate to the world of the book – although part of him already has.

My father wants to tell me about the drive and cleverness of the Germans, the seductive need to make better, the large abstractions that fuel the will, but he only looks up and says: "You should read this." The strength of his declaration startles me, alerts me to the tremors that might be waiting. Why I should read the book he doesn't say, nor do I ask. I know he cannot adequately express what the story means to him, or the way it might reverberate and create ripples in me. The eagerness and defensiveness and admiration and shame with which he meets William Shirer's words shimmer across the room. For a moment my mother puts down her knitting, the snow outside banking itself against spring.

I spend the short days of winter studying the washed-out sky, wondering if a crow will come to me, and what I might say to it. It won't speak to me the way my father's God spoke to those of His choosing. It keeps its bandit life but adds power now. Fed each day by the unhappy woman, it grows to understand who she is.

◆

Beyond the corral, the bush ends in a group of poplars. I don't notice them much in summer except sometimes to carve into their bark my DZ, careful lines that within the year become a grey-black blob of crust on the otherwise smooth skin with its greenish-white dust.

My father always notices when the first leaves appear, but each spring I miss them. One day the branches are bare, then the catkins form, my cue to pay attention; but every year the first unfurlings of green begin without my noticing. I see the green blush in the east bush first, high up where the light falls on the poplars' crowns. And when I look at the trees just past the corral, they too are beginning to turn green. I'm sure they must grow mostly in the night while I sleep, my window in the upstairs room open for perhaps the first time since winter.

It's winter that draws me to these trees. When the wind blows hard from the north, they catch the snow

THE FARM

drifting across the field unimpeded. At first there's only
a little snow at the base of the trees, but the drift grows,
and grows. I look out and watch the snow falling
through the cone of light spreading down from the yardlight. I want not just snow but wind, even though
walking home from school in that blast can hurt my feet,
my hands, my ears. Each morning I check how much the
drift has grown, until at last it has become a snowbank.

This winter the storms come so often the bank peaks
at fifteen feet. I crawl up its hard sides in my winter moc-
casins, kicking in toeholds. I mark the place on the trees
where the snow has reached. In spring I'll be able to look
up and see where once I stood. When the wind is hot
and the mosquitoes swarm up from the grass, I'll remember winter.

From that height I leap onto my toboggan and rocket
down the bumpy slopes and slide far out into the field,
stopped finally by the oat-straw stubble my forward
motion can't overcome. This first end point becomes
the measure of all other plunges down the bank. After
school and chores I climb the bank and push off, down
the hard snow and into the field. When I stop and look
back, the farm seems distant, sheltered by that curving
snowbank. I get up and plod back, breaking through the
crust with each step, until I'm back on the hard slope.
Up I go again, down I fly again, holding the curved front
of the toboggan.

It's the speed I like, the wind in my face, the distance
I cover, the way the farm seems left behind. But this
winter it's more than the speed: it's being fifteen feet off

25

the ground. I can look farther west than I could before. Up here the trees are skinny, more bendable, clean, too, no notches or marks on their bark. I'm as high as the opening in the barn's loft where we load the hay. From the loft, the yard and pastures and fences and granaries and fields seem strange, not smaller so much as less permanent. The loft becomes my place to hide, to look for the homes of the newborn kittens tucked back in corners under eaves where the hay is loose and hard to walk on.

When I climb to the top of the snowbank today, the afternoon turning darker, the sun already down but leaving behind enough light to see, I see that I'm higher than my father, who's working in the barn, doing the same chores that must be done over and over, day after day: feeding, cleaning, milking, waiting for winter to pass.

One more time I climb to the top, where I brandish a silver cap gun, shouting and swearing and ordering others to be brave. And knowing that when the bank melts away and leaves me back on the ground, I'll again be the shortest person around.

❖

The job of killing the kittens falls most often to my father. My mother is not afraid to bloody her hands beheading a chicken, and she's dispatched her share of the unwanted cats that arrive in the barn's hayloft, but this spring she withdraws to the house.

We are miles from the nearest farmer, who has enough

cats of his own. Nobody in town needs cats either, especially not farm cats so close to feral. We know farms where the cats have taken over the barns, howling and skinny. Some places are worse, with the cats in the house, drinking milk from dirty bowls and sprawling under the kitchen table.

This year, with my parents busy and my brothers working away from the farm, the job is suddenly mine. I'm last in the line of command; I know that role, but something has shifted. I'm no longer the special one, the protected one, coddled into great bursts of cocky brattiness. Now I'm the one who has to step up to new responsibility. I have no recourse. Perhaps my father has set this up; perhaps he knows some part of me wants this job. Maybe he knows that only someone so young can slaughter without scruples, crazy as only a kid can be, a craziness that will get the job done and carry me closer to the adolescents and adults around me.

I turn my mind to the actual task, the how of killing. I select the ground where I will bury them; I dig the hole in sandy soil behind the chicken coop. Back in the barn I fear I will bungle it, won't be able to carry through. The fascination – the draw – of cruel necessity nags at me, pulls me on.

I place fresh cream for the mother by the barn door and hurry up the ladder to the loft, to remove the kittens from their cozy nest before she returns and before they're old enough to open their eyes completely. I don't want them to see beyond their milkiness into my eyes. I leave only the black one with the white paw for the mother.

Gently (but why bother with gently now?) I place the other five in a grain sack and carry them to the hole in which they will be dropped. By me – I keep thinking it might not be me, someone will rescue me.

The kittens struggle against the jute weave of the sack. I plop them in the hole (not so gently now) and dump in a pail of water, hoping they will drown. But the water vanishes in the sand, leaving their small bodies wet and writhing. They plunge up and down against the jute. I throw on dirt, cover them. After three or four shovel-fuls there's no more sound or movement. I throw down the shovel and hurry away, marking the spot in my mind. I will never again dig there.

I go back to the barn. The mother looks crazy now she has only the one kitten. Her eyes are wide, fierce and yellow, and she looks up at me. I run out, call the dog and wander away to the field. I'm going to roll in the grass, or rub up against the big stone where the lichen makes a pattern of orange lace on its hard surface. I'll sit there, not thinking of much, while the dog digs around the edges looking for the mice and voles he likes to catch and shake in his large, watery mouth.

I keep pictures of birds, pictures I can look at for as long as I want, whenever I want; these are little cards in pack-ages of Red Rose tea. From the moment my mother shows me one, I'm enthralled by the beauty of the birds and the lust for collecting. All winter I wait patiently for the tea to be consumed and the new package to arrive. Others at school will be as keen as I am, I think, and we can trade cards.

I find that no one in the schoolyard cares about birds. I'm disappointed, but then realize I can get the kids to give the cards to me for nothing more than thanks. My mother helps me when she realizes, perhaps, that I've stumbled on one of my life's interests. She asks her friends to donate their cards, and soon I have the complete set of twenty-nine. I beg her to buy a frame so I can glue the cards onto cardboard and place them safely behind glass. She thinks I'm going too far now, but succumbs to my relentless begging. She buys a thin black frame with glass and cardboard backing for $2.50 from the Red & White store, and now I must decide how to arrange the birds. For the top row I settle on the eastern bluebird, purple martin, rose-breasted grosbeak, meadowlark, black and white warbler, and vesper sparrow. These are the best the artist, Louis Agassiz Guertes, has done.

Among the twenty-nine, I realize, there's no yellow-bellied sapsucker. He's not been captured by Guertes; is the bird not considered worthy, or is it too elusive to catch in paint? I've seen this bird often enough in the maple to know the markings on the head and throat, the dappled back and wings. Often he's on the fly, and I rarely get a satisfying look. I want to see him as clearly as I see the framed cards on my wall, the night hawk who bends his neck in flight to catch insects or the bobolink who displays on his beautiful back the colours usually found only on birds' breasts. I want a card of the sapsucker flying from the bush behind the shed, or landing on the trunk of the maple, or circling the tree like a woodpecker. He drills in the bark parallel rows of tiny bullet-like holes, returning later to feed on the sap that oozes and the insects caught in it.

The maple stands by the path between the house and the tractor shed. When I climb up into the tree, I can see beyond the roof of the shed and the old barn to the new barn, with its large square openings in the loft. If I pull myself up through the branches, I can almost reach the crown, hidden by the hand-sized leaves that hang everywhere, sticky with insect spit. Here I can spy. The shadow of a hawk glides by and sends the chickens running across the scratched-out ground for their coop.

Most of the trees that grow around our farm are poplars. They were cut and the stumps pulled when my grandfather cleared the land; they're the trees we cut each winter and haul in with the team of horses for firewood, stacking the long pale green bodies to dry; they're the ones that grow in the east pasture and create such a sameness of place I sometimes can't find my way home.

These poplars lack importance, unlike the cottonwoods my dad dug up from the far west ditch and planted in a row near the house, for shade in summer and relief from the icy wind in winter. My parents love the cottonwoods because they start growing the minute they're in the ground and rise to their spectacular heights and signal as far off as the road to town that here is a family that had the foresight to plant fast-growing, tall trees. These cottonwoods – like the lone maple planted when my grandmother was alive – have the status of the cultivated, as do the lilac bush, the caragana by the old house, and the crabapple and plum trees in the garden that were planted with such hope but that seldom produce decent, edible fruit.

The sapsucker prefers the maple. A quiet, unshowy bird, he's attracted to the sweetness of the tree, as I am. When the sap weeps out in spring, it forms little icicles that I break off in my mittens to suck, and the sugary cold and fuzzy wetness of the wool mingle to tell me soon I'll be able to walk again on thawed ground without the weight of winter overshoes. I often try to get a close look at the sapsucker but usually spot him only in flight, when he's about to disappear into the poplars.

One day I'm in the house when I hear a loud boom. I hurry out and see my father coming back to the house with the shotgun broken open across his arm. He says nothing but I know something is wrong. I hurry to the maple and find the sapsucker lying on his back in the dirt, his feet and claws – so good at hooking into bark – useless now. His eyes are closed. There's no blood on him that I can see. Dad used the scattershot to bring him down. I touch the soft feathers of his breast, which I see now are not really yellow but a muted beige. I admire the red feathers under his beak and on his crown, more intense than the colours in my card collection, more beautiful on the dead. I pick up the sapsucker and am surprised by his near weightlessness.

I can't think what should happen next. Should I bury him properly in the garden or throw him into the pile of manure and straw by the barn? Or leave him here on the ground for the bugs? Or pick him up by the feet and fling him into the bush, which is what I suppose my dad will do if he finds him here.

Instead, I carry him up into the maple. My father sided with the tree; for him there was no choice. But when I study this soft quiet thing in my hand, I'm not sure what I'd have done – maybe allowed him, over time, to ruin the tree. I hold him a while longer; then, in my secret perch up high, set him down in a small crook between limbs.

❖

The times I have to walk home from school, I face a choice. Head west on the new road to reach the curved road along the ditch and hope for a ride from someone going north out of town; or catch a ride north to Willie's corner, then walk west on the old road before turning the last half-mile north along our field. Most of the time I do what my brother does, but sometimes he's unwilling to wait for me or I'm on my own anyway, my lunch kit banging on my leg with every dusty step.

I take the old road even though there's no chance of getting a ride. Few cars pass here, the north end is high and wet, the clay catches your tires in spring and turns to hard ruts in summer. It's a half-forgotten stretch, travelled only now and then by Indians looking for the ditch to trap the beavers and muskrats. Sometimes farmers on tractors bounce their way along. One of our neighbours, Lorne, uses this road to walk his cow over to our bull.

When I reach the end of the road, I see a buggy going north. Two old men are sitting up front behind their two horses. All the farmers use horses for hauling up the stooks to the threshing machine and hauling away the cow manure into the fields, but I've never seen two men in a buggy like this one. I wonder why they don't use their car to go into town. Then it occurs to me: they don't have a car.

They stop for me. "Coming up?" asks the taller one, holding the reins. They move apart to let me sit between them. They're brothers or cousins, I think, because they look alike, same white bushy eyebrows and quiet way of joking. They smell alike too, sweetish, their Sunday clothes on, ties and coats even though it's Thursday and quite warm at that.

I can tell they like me, the level of their joking calculated to make me laugh. They're pleased to have a boy with them. Bobolinks beside us rise up out of my father's green wheat, then twist back down. The man with the reins tells his partner he's not the shortest man on the wagon after all, now that I'm here. I like the slow way the horses' rumps move, this way, then that. I like even better that I don't have to walk.

When they drop me off and I ask my mum who they are, she pauses a moment from rolling out dough for cinnamon buns. She can't quite remember. My dad says:

"Oh, those two, they're . . ." But he can't recall their names either, they have that far to go.

❖

Occasionally one of the Indians from the lake comes around in his humped-back old car, a woman inside with kids so quiet and big-eyed I guess they've never seen much. They seem to think we're the ones who are strange.

Their father shows us the pickerel he's caught in the big lake, good white fish so mouth-watering we always buy even if we've just gone to town and spent our money at the Red & White store. My dad seems to know him. Perhaps he's one of the Indians who come by at stooking time, when we can't get the work done by ourselves.

The only fish we get ourselves are suckers, fat fish that come in from Long Lake and Silver Lake along a little creek that flows into the west ditch. The creek doesn't have a name because nobody lives there. There's a sort of road that matches the creek, but it's mostly clay, and nobody drives there because there's no place to go and because the bridge that should connect it to the main road never got finished. What remains is pillars sinking into the mud on either side of the ditch, some bending and twisting, some still upright, and a few planks run across from pillar to pillar. If you want to reach the best place to catch suckers, you have to cross those planks.

When we reach the bridge, several cars are parked at the edge of the road where the gopher holes are apparently unoccupied. My dad crosses on the planks, and I follow, but I get stuck halfway. I feel the water rushing against the pillars, churning up through the wood and into the soles of my feet. I think if I take another step I'll upset the balance that's keeping me, just, from plunging into the water.

My dad is already on the other side. My mum is back with the other women on the road. She's talking and doesn't seem to notice I'm in trouble. I don't know who to call to. I don't want to call anyone because there are older boys here who went across without pausing. I'm thinking of my favourite rock at the edge of the field, not far from here, its orange lichen, how I like to lie on its curve and wait for the little mice and voles to come out from underneath. I'm thinking of the dog pouncing. I'm thinking of anything but here.

"What's the matter?" Dad asks, not in a gruff way, just telling me that I can continue on, speaking in such a patient, neutral way that I begin to think I can. I keep my eyes on my feet and slowly I start to move.

Dad reaches out and takes my hand when I get close, and I'm there, on solid ground again. I look back with satisfaction at those who aren't crossing over: the women, the little kids, the older people, the bachelors who stay and talk with the wives of other men. Suddenly they seem to belong to a different tribe altogether.

Then I'm running down to the creek to see the suckers. The creek is so narrow you can almost jump across. One man's stuffing fish into a grain bag, one after another, the bag jumping and twisting. Another's beating the water with willow branches. A tall boy uses a hay fork to pitch the fish onto the land where they wiggle and slide back into the water. He skewers one on his fork, holds it in the air like a flag. Yellow muck runs down the fork onto his hands. At first I think it's some kind of strange blood. Then I see it's eggs: these suckers are full of eggs. When the boy throws the fish to the ground and steps on it, he slips and falls. Everyone laughs.

I'm down by the water now, where the grass and clay are slippery. There's almost more fish than water. I see their big open mouths, their stupid-looking mouths. Someone has a chicken-wire net. He flings it into the water and hauls out more suckers. They keep coming, no matter that we're spearing and catching them. Someone's dog is here, barking and barking at the fish, caught up in the excitement.

My father has a sack with him, and he's pushing fish into it. "That's enough," he says, and starts back. I want to stay. Something will happen, I'm sure, because the men are laughing and shouting, bright-eyed. A couple are taking turns to see who can pitchfork the fish farther up on the bank. But I don't want to stay without Dad. I don't want to find myself crossing the planks when that dog decides it's time to go home.

We'll fry these suckers up just like the pickerel, I imagine, in butter with a little salt and pepper, browning the sides and eating them with bread. But when we get home, Dad doesn't take the fish into the house. Instead, he walks over to the chickens. Part of the yard around the coop has been closed off with snow fencing.

On the chickens' side, everything is dirt, scratched and pecked clean. He dumps the fish over the fence onto that dusty ground.

"We're not going to eat them?"

"They're too muddy-tasting," he says, then adds: "Some people like them."

The chickens come running. They don't stop to look, just sink their beaks into the fish. Before long, the dirt is all over the suckers, and in them, now that the chickens have opened up a cavity. They seem especially to like the gooey eggs.

I don't know if I would have crossed those planks if I'd known we were only fishing for the chickens. I like chickens when they're little, all fluffy and yellow in cardboard boxes from the hatchery. We keep them upstairs in the house at first, until they get strong enough to drink from the inverted bottles. I like to watch them, the way one of them starts peeping louder than the others when he seems lost.

But when they're older, when they get their feathers and the lice that comes with feathers, and we have to dust them and hold them upside down by their legs – then they're just farm work. They hop on one another. They peck one another's combs until one starts to bleed, and if we don't catch the bleeder in time and smear its comb with Peck-No-More, the others will just about kill it.

If the skunk doesn't get into the coop at night and kill them, one after another, Dad hauls them to the market in the truck, where they're killed anyway (except for the time he brought them back because the market man offered him only ten cents a chicken). But even then I don't feel sorry for them.

It's the fish I feel sorry for. I'm wondering if they might have made it down the ditch and into the big lake. Maybe they would have turned into pickerel when they got there. Instead they end up here, dead. The way the chickens are pecking, it's as if these fish are the last thing they'll eat before Mum catches one.

She takes it to the chopping block. She brings down the axe and then throws the headless bird well away so the blood won't spurt on her clothes. The soundless chicken flops around the yard, twisting and turning and slowing down. The dogs are there to investigate, of course, sniffing at the block and at the chicken head lying there with its dainty eyelid closed. But nobody eats a chicken head – not a dog, not even another chicken.

❖

I'm cranky as only a kid can be, and my list of grievances is long: too many times lately I've had to walk that mile and a half home from school. The trucks and cars throw up gravel dust in my face as I hug the edge of the road between the vehicle and the ditch, and they give me no thought and no wave. I have no luck with neighbours who all seem to be in a hurry to get home, as I am. Not much is waiting for me: my dog, my mother, maybe her fresh rolls. Then work: chores with the yard and the animals, homework, more chores, gardening, then . . .

It doesn't seem like my life at all. I know what life is

supposed to be. I yearn to get away to somewhere else where my real, true life can begin. I imagine it as I walk along the road, kicking stones into the water or throwing sticks at the muskrats that live in the nearly vertical banks of the ditch.

My new world isn't quite in focus yet. It certainly involves less time doing chores. I have a fantasy about a young boy who lives by himself under the stairs in his uncle's house, so there's someone to watch out for him if need be, but he's on his own, settled in, the cramped space his first independent lodging. He hangs up calendar pictures and his framed bird pictures, he sets up a little card table, he never cooks. Food appears, dishes vanish and return – essentials, never more than that. He's sure he wants to live this life, clean and orderly and free from demands. His little bed is a mattress on the floor, and sometimes his uncle's dog comes to lie beside him, but no one is ever allowed in.

I'm finally home, the day is through, and then it's another day and then suddenly it's Sunday, a good Sunday, not one of the days we trudge off to church and sit through gloomy sermons and mournful hymns. It's a sleep-in Sunday, but I'm nagging my mother, and before I know it my tone is out of control, my complaints and whining directed at her: she's the reason the world is so stupid; she's the reason my feelings confuse me. Why can't she just fix it; she's the one who *had* me, the one to blame.

In a moment my father is standing over me – I'd forgotten him – and he's gripping my face in his left hand while the right has a fistful of my shirt. "Don't you talk to your mother like that!"

I can see his teeth are bad. Abruptly I get perspective, and shake out of his grasp and flee the house, working hard to hold back tears. Where did they come from so suddenly? Where did *he* come from so suddenly?

My mother finds me in the garden and tries to explain. I don't really hear her words so much as the soothing sound of her voice. She tells me my father loves me, I have to believe this. Then she's saying something different; her tone changes and seems directed more towards herself than to me: "I'm always the one who has to talk to him for you kids." She's the go-between, and tired of that role; and although she's not actually telling me I have to go talk to my dad now on my own, I realize that my doing so would lift a burden off her shoulders.

At first I can only glimpse what she proposes. In my mind my father and I are talking to each other comfortably. But he's old, and when he's tired, he stoops: what can he say to me? There's distance between us, and shyness: we've been here before. There have been other explosions, rare but remembered. Now we have to work our way back together, find a balance. But how, when I can't talk to him and he won't talk to me?

We meet over some task at the forge, that bellowing hot machine in the tractor shed. I turn the handle to fan the coals until they glow. My father bends low. He picks up a spike in the pincers and thrusts it into the coals until it glows pink and then white. Then he pulls it from the heat and hammers it, hard ringing clangs that fill the shed with waves that pass right through me. A half-dozen hits, and then he sticks it in a pail of water and the steam clouds up in an acrid scream.

He repeats these dance-like movements, bending, banging, and waiting, and I watch and help as I can, and all around us the smell of the forge and the anvil, the metal fumes in the air that taste of blood.

When Miss Prawdsik tells us about the eclipse, I know I want to remember and pay attention. I try to imagine it happening right now. With Theresa on my left and the other David on my right, we're doing penmanship exercises, making only Os across the page. I'm alert to the moment when they will all lift their heads to look outside as the poplars across the schoolyard bend, the light wrong, weak and frightening.

This is the summer Dad thinks I'm old enough to pick mustard weeds out of the wheat. The tallest plants are already green past my knee and starting to produce seed heads. When I raise my arms and stick them straight out like a scarecrow's, I picture four times that distance on either side; that's the width of the swath I take through the field. I keep my feet in the rows to avoid stepping on the wheat.

I zigzag across my space, pulling up mustard plants. I hold them in my arms like a bouquet, a prickly, smelly, spitbug-ridden bouquet that requires me to wear long sleeves even though it's over 90 degrees. Now would be a good time for the eclipse to lower the light and maybe freshen the breeze; then maybe I could walk through forty acres of wheat and pick every yellow-headed weed. Dumping the bundle at each end of the field is the rule, but sometimes I lay it down in mid-field; sometimes I merely twist off the heads, so their flowers will not show themselves to my father when he comes to inspect how much I've done.

Summer also means I can drag the tin tub out to the house pump and fill it with water strangely cold. Once the sun turns the water warm, I can hop in and out all afternoon, turning brown. The rest of my family comes and goes from the house, to the barn and to the fields, while I play in the tub. The sun burns the top of my feet quickly. I feel its blaze on my shoulders. The dog comes over, and I splash him, and he goes away to sleep in the shade. Doesn't he know he'll miss the eclipse if it comes now?

On the day of the eclipse a neighbour has driven into the yard. He and my dad have gone to look at a stack of bales behind the barn. I come up to hear what they're saying – they're talking not about the hay but about the eclipse. And sure enough, just then, the light begins to dim, the air around us thickens. I breathe differently. I want the sky to become so dark we'll need to turn on the yardlight.

Our neighbour is a thin man I don't know well. He's wearing overalls so baggy he could hang himself up by a stick in the field. His face, however, is kind and not frightening. He peers down at my father and says: "I guess it's about that time of year."

An eclipse doesn't happen every year, it's not like my birthday. I'm surprised to see a man, an *adult*, who doesn't know what Miss Prawdsik has taught us: an eclipse is a special moment. Someone his age should know. I'm only a kid, and I know. Perhaps he never learned about the moon blocking out the midday sun – but then what else doesn't he know? And how many others don't know and are just pretending?

In Dad's face I see a brightness, as if he's enjoying this great event. But I'm scared it'll get so dark I won't be able to find him. Our neighbour and I will have to listen as he guides us with his voice back past the bales and into the barn where he can throw on the lights.

I want to reach out but realize I don't have to: the eclipse will soon be over, and Dad will look as he always does. When I think of the dark, he's not there. But when I think of fields full of wind and light, I see him, up to his waist in the grain, cap tight on his forehead, bending down to examine his crop as grasshoppers fly off the stems, a pair of crows drifting past, one big hawk sitting in the fringe of poplars where my initials are carved in a tree trunk and where the field, full of weeds and hope, comes to an end.

❖

When the piglets are born, when they come squirting out of the rear end of the sow who lies there grunting calmly, they're cute. Half helpless, with a clean smell that takes a while to leave them, and with little black alert eyes. Dad says they're smart, and I believe him. But sometimes the mother rolls onto one of the newborns and kills it, so instead of twelve piglets there are eleven. Or half kills it, stepping on it, her hooves cutting right through into its guts, the high-pitched squeals upsetting the sow even more.

Dad has to come and take the wounded one away. If he thinks it might live, he brings it to the house and puts it in a box lined with an old flannel shirt behind the stove, where we take turns feeding it with a bottle. It doesn't smell like the barn, not that bad at all, but my mum doesn't like competition for her baked-bread aroma even though she's sorry for the damaged thing, especially if it's the runt. If Dad thinks the piglet's too badly hurt, he does something with it behind the barn. He doesn't let me see what.

I like the pigs when they're little, the way they run so fast once they venture out of the barn. The sow is not allowed out, so I bring clumps of sod for her to root her snout into. She pushes the sod around her pen, keeping it either beside the trough or near the straw where she sleeps, never pushing it into the corner where she shits. I wonder if she remembers how she herself once ran the way her babies run, around the corner of the barn and into the field where they push their own noses into the dirt and fling it into the air, then kick and twist their hindquarters just for the fun of it. Or flop down into the puddles after a rain and leap out to run again, half pink, half black, like little pintos. Each time they're outside, they venture farther from their mother. Once I came upon them in the back field, past the garden, by the north well. We surprised each other.

How they squeal when Dad cuts their teeth. Their little tusks are sharp and the sow won't put up with them when they bite her teats while sucking. Dad grabs one out of the pen, pulling it up by a hind leg, flipping it over on its back and holding it between his knees.

"I'm not going to hurt you, oh no," he says. "I'm not going to hurt you at all."

The piglets squeal and wiggle, then turn quiet when Dad pries open the mouth and snips with pliers. They don't know he's on their side, he's the one who gets them to life in the first place by bringing the big boar over from Lorne's. He's also the one who gives them the needle, so they don't get erysipelas and die. I watch when he sticks it behind the right front leg and a little sack of fluid builds up.

I don't get to watch when, later, the males are castrated. They're hardly big enough to know what's happening. Their little balls are just beginning to bulge out when Lorne comes again. Once more they're caught, flipped, and cut. I hear the squeals differently this time. I see them coming out of the barn one by one with their slits smeared with something that looks like iodine. Later I try not to notice when the dogs find the little round bits in the manure pile and gulp them down.

When the piglets are fed deworming powder, they're listless for a day, lying among the long ribbons of dead tapeworms. By the time spring's over, they're on their own, eating and sleeping side by side, head to bum in the sun, sometimes in the mud in the shade of the old pig barn, where the rats have their nests under the broken boards.

Sometimes the dogs flush out a rat. What a surprise when they discover it's not a mouse. The rat turns its teeth on the dog's nose in that last moment before it's bitten to death and left on the path to the chop house for me to come upon without warning, my eye drawn more to the long naked tail than to the fat body and small mangled head.

One day Dad says: "It's time to kill the rats." He mixes chopped-up oats with cement and Paris green and water, and places this mixture in troughs off the floor where the pigs won't find it, because of course they would eat it. He puts the troughs up on the poles that run from one wall to another, a makeshift roof covered with straw to help the pigs keep warm in winter. That straw is dead and musty, held down by dust and pigeon droppings coming from the upper loft. When I have to crawl onto this straw to look for the nest of a broody hen who won't lay her eggs in the chicken coop, I think I'd rather be one of those many-coloured birds with weird eyes flying back and forth to the grain elevator in town. On hands and knees in the rats' territory, I move as weightlessly as I can. I don't want to surprise them out of their holes.

The morning after the poisoning, I see rats flopping, cement hardened in their guts, poison tightening on their brains. One walks along the rafters, slowing down until it stops, then falls off, dead. I think we might be rat-free now, but I still can't open the door to the chop house without bracing for scuttling near the hole. The hole reminds me of what once lived here, what might return, one old smart one who tried to warn the others not to eat the easy food. He's biding his time under the boards, waiting for the pigs to sleep, so he can come out and find in the corners of the trough the bits of grain the pigs can't scoop up with their snouts.

The pigs have nothing to do all summer but fatten up for fall. My dad sees them as dollars by now, so much a pound. He might sell them as weanlings or keep them through the winter. We sometimes have two, even three generations in different pens. By the time I'm back in school in September, he's listening to the noon stock report closely and drinking his Red Rose tea, the numbers for pork running through his head.

❖

My mother grows peas and corn and cucumbers and tomatoes and carrots in her garden. Bending from the waist, the brim of her wide straw hat nearly sweeping the ground, she weeds the portulaca that grows better than the vegetables. We eat from her garden right through the winter because she preserves the vegetables, blanching them and storing them in the freezer. When she cans, she begins early in the day, "to beat the heat," she says, getting the wood stove in the kitchen burning hot, moving the blue enamel canner around to find the right temperature, inserting the glass jars full of vegetables into the boiling water, extracting them with a claw-like apparatus that enables her to set them down on the counter, where they're covered with a cloth to keep them cozy. All day she listens for the pinging of the lids as they get sucked down, sealed. At night when she removes the cloth to check them, she taps the centre of each lid. When she finds one that has not sealed, she says, "That bugger," and laughs, glancing at me.

My father does not help in the garden, but the potato crop belongs to both of them. Early red Pontiacs are grown near the house, and the later white Netted Gems occupy the field. We use special seed potatoes; my father shows me how to push the eye into the dirt. In no time at all, the plants come up through the clods of soil. I sit on my heels, wondering how the little plants find their way. I think of the freshness of new potato, but when I dig under one of the plants I find nothing. I settle instead for rhubarb flourishing wild at the edge of the bush. Dipped in white sugar, the sour stalk tastes as fresh, if not as satisfying, as new potatoes. Dad tells me you can't rush potatoes, they grow on top first, down below later.

In early summer he hitches Flip, the more patient of our two horses, to the cultivator and steers her through the rows. She tries to keep her front hooves off the plants. Dad wrestles with the reins and the cultivator, forcing its blade down into the dirt. He wants to overturn or bury the mid-row weeds and provide mounds for the potatoes. In fall we set aside a day to unearth them and haul them back to the house in sacks. I try to follow my dad's way of tying twine around the necks of the grain bags. He threads the twine in and out of his little finger, then pulls until the twine squeaks. We dump the potatoes rumbling down into the cellar next to the coal bin and the cistern. During the winter my mum will pick out the ones caved in by rot. She takes these to the pigs, who squeal and compete at the trough for the pleasure of any kind of slop.

Sometimes I stay behind in the cellar. Here are the rows of pickled cucumbers and beets, the dark tall bottles of homemade chokecherry wine. There's the table where Dad saws up the hind quarter of deer and Mum wraps up the meat in shining brown paper, writing with a grease pencil "roast" or "steak" and the date.

Down here must be where the dark comes from. I lie in my bed on the top floor and finally have to call my mother, my first plea a half-test against the night, the second growing louder because I know she can't hear me yet. Before she comes, my brother, in the next room, yells at me: "Go to sleep!" It's hard for him to forgive me for waking him up. He's only just got home from the dances, only just fallen asleep – and there are all those forkfuls of hay Dad's expecting him to lift into the barn.

Down in the basement, in winter, I touch the long pale feelers that creep out from the spuds stored under the coarse weave of the sacks. What dim light finds its way into their cobwebbed corner?

My birthday's next month, but it feels as if we're celebrating already because we're having pancakes, my second-favourite way to eat potatoes, second only to raw, peeled and salted. My mum gets me to scrape potato after potato into a bowl. "Watch your knuckles," she warns. The watery white and brown mess rises slowly in the bowl. The little triangular bits that I can't grate any further I pop into my mouth. I taste the soupy mix on the ends of two fingers. Then my mum grates in an onion. She wipes her eyes with the corner of her apron.

My brother and I compete to see who can eat more pancakes. We're at eight now. My mother hands the golden pancakes to us from the stove as they're done, one to him, one to me. We slather on brown sugar, watch it melt, add some butter – butter I made yesterday, cranking the churn, getting cranky that the cream was not turning fast enough – and then cut them into pieces, eating more slowly now. Nine, ten, eleven. When we finally reach twelve apiece, my mother sits down and eats.

My brother gets up to flip the pancakes at the stove. When he returns to the table, I mimic him. When he cuts, I cut. When he puts down his fork, so do I. If he reaches for sugar, I wait till he's finished sprinkling it, then I reach for sugar, too. After a while he realizes what I'm doing. He glances at me. I gawk right back. He's trying to think of a move I can't copy, or better still, one that will lead me down the path to my father.

When he gets up, I get up. When he comes back to the table, I come back. I'm smiling and smiling. My mother smiles too: she knows what I'm up to.

"Pass the butter," my brother says. My father pushes it across the table.

When he's finished, I say: "Pass the butter." He ignores me, trying not to laugh.

My mother and brother and I are nearly giggling. My

dad finally catches on, raises his head, and starts to laugh, too. That's when I get out of hand, now that he's on my side. I exaggerate every move my brother makes. I want to jump up and push my hands into his chest. He's growing away from me, and I don't like to be left behind. I don't like this natural way of things. We once were friends, and for years we slept in the same bed, sharing our breath on cold nights.

Thirteen, fourteen, fifteen pancakes. The birthdays when he shot up, paid attention to his hair. I won't be able to stick with him much longer.

He wins at sixteen: I can't eat one more pancake. He pushes back from the table and goes upstairs to lie on his bed. I've seen him up there, staring at the ceiling. He wins again. I can't copy him. I can't lie still that long.

How my dad selects which pig to kill I don't know. They've all been fed the same mixture of chopped oats and water, along with slop from the house – potato peels, corncobs, carrot tops, wash water – and they all complain so noisily at the trough you would think we hadn't just fed them that morning. They all look the same to me, not like the cows with their differences of brown and white and personality. One pig might be a little bigger than another, but they all have that same rounded back, those floppy ears we have to check for sunburn, that wrinkled snout that's capable of eating almost anything. I know, because once I saw them corner an old hen.

One day Fritz comes with his big truck. He's a gentle man with thick white hair and a calmness that must come from hauling so many animals to the meat packers: calves, cows, steers, an occasional horse, now pigs. I've seen him pushing a calf, twisting its tail until its eyes bulge and it shits wildly, its hooves slipping on the slimy truck deck. Pigs are easier to move, more likely to run up the ramp together. As the circle of men in the pen grows tighter and the pigs' squeals louder, one pig makes a dash up the ramp. Soon the others follow, the gate in the back of the truck is dropped, and they're on their way.

Each pig gets a whack from Fritz's hammer, a stamp that tells him which farmer this pig belongs to when he pulls into the auction. Dad's sure he's only raising A-grade pigs, and when he finds out later that one of them was sold as B-grade, he gets mad, saying something to himself I can't make out. But it's too late, the pigs are gone.

Except for the one he's chosen for us. He waits for a cool fall day when the flies have died. He prepares early in the morning, hauling buckets of water heated on the kitchen stove and dumping them into a big barrel. The barrel sits on stones, where he makes a fire and gets the water scalding hot. He crawls up into the loft of the old pig barn and attaches a pulley to the centre beam. Then he goes into the house, where he sharpens his German knives and loads the .22. We don't kill a pig every fall, so this is a special occasion. It has some of the same excitement as my birthday.

When he calls the pig over to the trough, I think there might be a moment when he hesitates. Or perhaps it's not hesitation so much as prayer; I don't know. Then he reaches over the fence and scratches the pig's ears and shoots it between the eyes. It drops without a sound, back legs kicking. My dad's over the fence into the pen. He sticks his knife — the long cutting knife from the kitchen — into its neck, but even though the pig is flabby with fat, the hide is tough. He has to force the blade until blood finally spurts onto the mud. It doesn't take long for the legs to stop moving. The eyes half close.

Often a neighbour comes to help. He and Dad drag the pig over to the beam. My dad cuts the skin at the back of the legs and slips the hooks from a singletree under the tough tendons. Everyone pulls on the rope to lift the pig into the air, but my dad pulls hardest. Slowly we raise the pig off the ground, its hind feet spread by the singletree jammed under its tendons, its nose still dripping blood onto the stones of the barnyard.

The dogs are circling now. We chase them away, but the smell of blood draws them back. Dad pulls the pig higher, then lowers it into the barrel of hot water, then pulls it out again. Once more it goes in, head first, again and again until the heat softens the hair and scaly dirt on its skin. The neighbour has a different idea.

"Alfie, just burn the hair off," he says, trying to convince Dad to singe the pig's skin with a torch. But Dad says the meat tastes bad then, smoky in the wrong way. Finally the men begin scraping at the hide. I know this isn't like shaving, but I can't help but think of it when I see my dad later in the week at the mirror, scraping his neck with the razor.

Once the pig is clean, clean like it's not been since the day it was born, Dad kicks a large tub into place beneath the dangling head. He unfolds his good knife, reaches up to make the first cut. He starts at the top, near the tail, in the underbelly where the skin looks soft. Slowly he opens the pig, cuts out the anus, and pulls gently at the intestines, cutting away the gristle that sticks to the sides and back of the cavity. He's careful not to cut the bulging tubes because he doesn't want shit on his hands or on the meat. Out come the bladder, kidneys, liver, steaming in the cool air; the lumpy stomach, and some bright green part that Dad tells me is where the bile comes from. Then the rubbery pink lungs, the dark red heart, the veins, bits and pieces I don't recognize. All of it drops down into the tub, the many tones surprising me. I had thought our insides were all one colour, like blood, maybe, or darkness.

We can rest, now that the animal's turned from itself into something else. Cut into pieces, stored in the freezer, this is not the animal we watched being born, the one we laughed at when it ran, the one we faithfully fed and fed. We hang the chunks of bacon in the smoke-house. Only oak bark will provide the right kind of smoke. We don't have oak fence posts of our own, but we strip bark from those of a neighbour. The loss of bark doesn't weaken the posts, and perhaps my dad asks the neighbour first. When the oak is burning, we smother the flames with sawdust and the place fills with smoke. We keep that smoke going for weeks. Soon I'll be able to cut off strips with my jackknife, chewing on the rich flavoured meat as I go about my winter chores.

We use as much of the pig as we can, but we're not like the really poor families who blow up the bladder for a ball. And I'm glad we no longer use Grandma's recipe for a pig's-feet meal. It's hard not to remember where those feet have been. Sometimes Mum boils the fat on the stove, rendering, she calls it, adding lye and letting the mix harden.

It's this soap she uses in the wringer washer when Dad comes from cleaning the pig barn. Pig shit and straw have been trampled into a thick mat he can lift only by working it with his two-pronged pick, slowly loosening it and rolling it back towards him like a rank carpet. It's a hard job, and he's in the pen for hours. When he comes to the house, Mum says: "Don't come in here smelling like that." He takes off his shit-smelling clothes in the porch, not far from where the pig's head is waiting for Mum to cut the meat out of its jowls for head cheese, its tiny dead eyes watching my father undress.

# — THE FIVE MILES TO TOWN —

The dentist comes to town twice a year, spring and fall. He smiles as he unloads his leather bags from his long maroon car, newer than the ones our fathers drive, cleaner, too, as if he's come here on roads that aren't dusty. He sets up a temporary office in one of the ground-floor rooms of the Corona Hotel, the tallest building in town not counting the grain elevator, which is so tall it doesn't count. From the bench in the entryway we can look up the carpeted stairs to the second-floor rooms. No one ever stays in those rooms except Dr. Boyd, now and then a straggler blown off course, maybe an extra relative at a family reunion who couldn't be accommodated at the farm. Otherwise the place is empty, haunted by the people who aren't there.

Off the entryway is a room of stuffed birds, their dust tickling my nose. Pheasants and prairie chickens stand on shelves attached to the wall, and one white owl under a bell jar regards me with his immovable eye. I've never been so close to such a bird, although I've seen one perched on a fence post. The other birds seem nonchalant about their new lives at the Corona Hotel, but the snowy owl tells me he is not pleased. I touch the glass, and understand why he's protected from fingers such as mine. I want to poke his soft shape, feel the grip of talons on my finger before I lift him into flight.

The bird room is off limits to me – to any of Dr. Boyd's patients – but I sneak under the cord. In the other direction is a large, dark, smelly, smoky room. Men come here to drink, and get drunk. My father never goes there, never. My mother, of course, isn't allowed, and even if she were, she wouldn't consider it. To think some men come in from their fields before the day is done and sit down with a beer! I've been taught to recognize such acts as false comfort.

Mr. Post is in charge – of the beer parlour, the travelling dentist, the hotel – and he must also look after his wife, an apparition who shuffles through the halls and rooms in her bedroom slippers, a frayed housecoat held half-heartedly tight at her neck. She seems to have given up on daily life as not worth considering. She glares down at those of us unlucky enough to be sitting in her entryway, as if surprised to find us here. Sometimes she has a scarf wrapped around her black hair; other times it flies wildly. When she comes out from their private rooms, we push back against the wall.

Of all the people I know, Mrs. Post is the only one who has no variations of history. She's always been this way — sometimes fierce, sometimes so languid she's almost sleeping — and we never know which way she'll be. I can't pry information from my parents. Being strange means she's free from having to change. I worry that she will notice me or catch me in the bird room. My family is distantly related to her: my father's older sister married her brother. I know they have money, but money doesn't seem to help her.

My mum and dad both have bad teeth, so bad they don't go to the dentist. My father has stumps here and there, stained from the snuff he enjoys sticking under his tongue. When he drives, he spits out the window, and his snoose dribbles down the side of the car. This habit we have the most trouble loving. My mother's teeth are better, and she hopes eventually they'll both be able to afford new ones. Meanwhile they have to pay attention to the kids, whose teeth are more important than their own.

One of the Wilson boys turns blue in Dr. Boyd's chair, and by the time he's taken to the nearest hospital, two hours away, he's dead. I'm shocked and hungry for details of what must be this year's most gruesome death. Every year we have our share, the latest a man trying to unplug the wet straw from inside his throbbing combine. But death by dentist is unusual even for us.

I learn what I can, discover the family didn't know their son was allergic to anaesthetic. Before Dr. Boyd comes to town again, many of his patients decide it's best to drive the two hours to Neepawa. My family is not among them. My parents must have discussed the pros and cons of sending their children to someone who has inadvertently killed the son of neighbours. Either they're unwilling to drive the distance to Neepawa, or they can block out the sound of the mother who keeps saying all over town: "He's a butcher." As if any more evidence of his misdeeds were needed, my sister tells me that when she goes in, he locks the door behind her and strokes her cheek in a way she doesn't like, and doesn't use freezing.

When it's my turn, Dr. Boyd stands at the door and calls me down. I go in alone, settle myself in his big leather chair. In front of me a window looks onto the train station; beside me is a tray of steaming instruments and the drill he starts by hand, yanking the pulley and keeping it working with his foot pedal. Sometimes the drill catches in my tooth, stalls, and must be started most awfully without being removed from its deepest penetration into the rot. A can on the floor holds white cloths with blood splotches.

The smell of dental torment is a reassuring laundered one, the starched white jacket Dr. Boyd wears. When he presses my head against the bulk of his gut, I smell the cleanness and feel the stiffness of his uniform on my cheek. He looks into my mouth and I look at his large bald head, the mottled red tint of his skin, that ferocious smile. He mutters to me: "You've been eating too much candy, haven't you," and of course it's true, my family loves peppermints and Life Savers.

My failure to stop eating candy allows him to punish me. His forehead gleams. His arm comes up and around before I see the needle. I cannot shout because my mouth is full of fingers. I taste soap and then the quick bitterness of the freezing. Even if I could yell, my cry would be deadened by the silence of the empty hotel; my companions awaiting their turn would hear nothing.

By the time he's done with me, my mother has arrived. She opens her purse and takes out her money. She always pays cash. She talks with Mrs. Post, who happens to be near. The three of them – Mum, Dr. Boyd, Mrs. Post – stand chatting near the darkness of the private rooms, Dr. Boyd taller than my mother, shorter than Mrs. Post, his smile intact. I wonder if he sleeps with it in place, up in one of those empty rooms, dreaming of driving back to wherever he lives. He must live somewhere; he can't spend all his time on the road, finding patients like me and the dead Wilson boy.

I linger, wanting to go outside, until I can wait no longer. I throw open the door and leap down the steps into the street where I spit and spit, waiting for my mother to offer me a mint to ease the hurt in my mouth and cut the metallic taste.

❖

The summer I drive to the Calgary Stampede with my parents and uncle and his family, I return home desperately wanting a horse. I had no idea desire could bloom so fiercely. I will be changed from the child I don't want to be into a cowboy. I watch the way they ride their horses and slap their worn jeans with their hats. I notice that they move in a silence wonderfully unlike the one that surrounds my father, and the idea of who I will be moves west.

By the end of our first day's travel I note changes: the trees disappear completely, the licence plates become a different colour – but the sun and the wind don't change. One morning I smell something new in the air outside the motel where we've spent the night, a new kind of weather, something damp and rich. By the following afternoon I'm looking into big gullies cut through by rivers. The dirt at the B/A station where we stop is the same gravel and dust we have at home, but beyond the parking lot the earth looks red. We've all been excited to see the antelope and the occasional big hawk, but no one says anything about the new feeling in the air. When I look up now, I expect to see some new dazzle.

I do. We drive between sandy humps rising on either side of the highway. The horizon comes and goes, sometimes blocked by the hills around us. Then from the top of one hill I glimpse at last the mountains of snow, even though it's summer. When we arrive at my dad's cousins' in the foothills, I never want to think about farming again. When I step outside that first morning, the air smells clean and cool, with a trace of snow coming down from the mountains to meet me.

That's when I meet Lady, the quarterhorse my relatives ride around their ranch when they bring in the cows. Cattle, they call them. I'm lifted into the saddle. How wide my legs must spread! When Lady walks, her neck bobs up and down. She's got spirit but I'm allowed only to walk her back and forth in the yard. I'm not sure I have the knack of neck-reining, which seems the opposite of logic. I convinced my mum I had to have a Stetson, and even if it's not the real felt thing, its intermeshing straw is close enough. I wear it on Lady, imagining how I will look with the right kind of jeans: confident, upright, knowing I'll soon be galloping on my own.

When we go to the Stampede, everywhere I see men I wouldn't mind becoming. They have boots with heels, big buckles, hankies, hats. They walk as if they've got the time to get where they're going. They stick their boots through the corral fence, turn to talk quietly to one another without lifting their arms off the top railing. Even when they're riding a bronco that's bucking wildly, twisting and leaping, these men seem gentle. When they're yanking down a steer by its horns and driving it into the dirt, they seem kind. They know exactly who they are. They don't want to be anything other than the cowboys they were born to be.

My hat is great, and I can probably get the belt, and the hanky won't cost Mum much. But I know she's not going to buy the jeans or the boots. I've seen the prices, I know. We're already spending more than we have by coming this far west. The boots are necessary for safe riding, I could make a good case, but even if my mum would buy them I'm not sure I could wear them back home. The other kids would laugh at me. They won't understand because they haven't seen the shining mountains, the horses, the rolling hills, the cowboys. They'd be stuck in that hot air on a flat bush farm.

Every time I see a cowboy up close, lugging a saddle or wiping down a hot horse, I study him. Some of them are young, not much older than my brothers, but already they have those lines around their eyes that tell me they've crossed over into being men.

After lunch at the Stampede grounds, my dad and I go to the men's washroom. I wait for him to come out of one of the cubicles. Other men come and go. I notice one man with a cowboy's leather vest standing at the urinal shaking himself. Then I see he's still shaking himself, and realize what he's doing. He half looks back over his shoulder to see if anyone's watching, but his attention isn't really there. The big boys at my school have been graphic in their demonstrations, I know what he's doing. I'm surprised that grown-ups do it. I know it's not something you do here.

I can't take my eyes off him. It's like the first time I saw the Rockies: I had to look for a long while because I feared things would change if I dared look away. The other men at the long row of urinals have left. He's up there on his own now. I can't tell if he's hoping that nobody notices or that somebody will.

My dad tugs my arm. "Come on. Are you ready?"

He knows. He's seen it, too, but he's not going to say anything. And I'm not going to say anything. This is not something we will ever talk about. The closest we'll get is the moment just past, the moment our eyes met. I hadn't realized what could be said without words. Even with all their skills and know-how, these cowboys wouldn't be able to signal through a single glance not just embarrassment and disapproval but something else, some reassurance and comforting acknowledgment of the emptiness I'm feeling.

I stop wanting to be a cowboy after that. Three weeks later, back home, I don't feel the urge to get those special clothes. I still have my straw hat, but it seems big on my head. I do remember Lady fondly, the power she had, the way she obeyed me immediately when I touched the reins. I remember the smell of her, the strength of her, the body built for speed, not for hauling, the delicacy of her legs and the strangeness of her iron shoes, the fancy shiny bit and the special way it went into her mouth and its potential for cruelty that I was quick to grasp.

But Lady isn't here. The closest thing is Flip, our black mare, or Patch, our brown and white gelding. They're in the far corner of the pasture, where water seeps in under the fence from the neighbour's slough and makes a green edge. When the cows pass through it, mud squirts up through their hooves and onto their white ankles. Sometimes, after the white-faced Herefords have finished eating for the morning, the sun burns down on their broad leather backs and they venture into the mud, their bellies almost in the water. I like being out here, especially in spring, when I float my homemade boats and throw stones at the ducks bobbing back and forth under the wire fence.

Today, though, the water is gone, and the cows are in the west pasture. I've come to ride Flip. She isn't Lady; she's not the kind of horse you ride; she's meant to haul and pull. Patch is younger but too strong for me. I know better than to try to climb on him. He would buck me off and give a hard nip with his big yellow teeth as I went down.

I take Flip by the halter and lead her to the water trough. I slide the bridle into her mouth. She doesn't seem to mind when I slip the straps over her ears. One foot on the edge of the trough, I talk sweetly to her and then heave myself onto her back. Up here she's wider than she seems from the ground. Higher too. I have to spread my legs so wide, even wider than I did on Lady, I know they're going to hurt before long.

Flip doesn't move, just stands patiently, waiting, I realize, for me. Patch is the one that starts, stepping away from us, shaking his head up and down so his mane waves. When I prod Flip with my heels, it feels as if she moves first her right side and then her left. It's hard to find the place to sit: up near the mane is too hard, down in the middle all sway, back near the rump too tricky.

I dig my heels in and she jerks forward. I pull at the reins, trying not to hurt her mouth. She begins to trot, and I begin to bounce. I have to work her into a canter if I'm going to enjoy this ride, but she seems unable to move her vast bulk any faster. I dig my heels deeper, urge her on. At last she lifts into that smooth roll. Actual wind blows in my face.

Every day I come out to ride her. Sometimes I have to trick her with a pail of grain because when she sees me with the bridle, she turns and walks away. I ride her in the middle of the afternoon when Dad is on the cultivator, because I don't think he'd like to see me pushing her the way I must to get that rolling canter. Every day she fights me more, not bucking, just shaking her head, trying to take the bit in her teeth. Sometimes I have to pull hard to make her obey.

I see I'm going to have to leave her alone, not just because she doesn't like me on her but because she can't take me where I want to go. I'm beginning to think staying home is better than going away because going away means wanting to be somebody I can't be when I get back. I can't really remember the Stampede now, or how much I wanted to be a cowboy. I can't even quite picture the cowboy at the urinal or the look in my dad's eye. Next month, when the teacher asks me how I spent my summer holidays, I'll have to find something else to say.

Everyone seems to have at least one fat uncle, and sometimes mine visits with his skinny wife. He's without her this time, in my mother's kitchen, wearing his brown hat with earflaps, beige vest with rows of special pockets for the fat shotgun shells (usually red although occasionally dark blue) with their special powder for the high-flying birds. He's climbed out of his waders to stand on my mother's linoleum, his feet wrapped in thick wool socks.

He and my dad have had a good hunt. Six mallards are lying outside on the grass, where the dogs are smelling them and being shooed away by my father. They're not the local hang-about ducks but big northern flyers that have winged their way down from the summer tundra, perfect birds, fed on the long summer light and not yet depleted by the hard flight south. The heads of the males are glowing green, their necks turned at the restful angle they earned by taking a wingful of lead and plummeting to the swampy ground near the makeshift blind my father and uncle leaped from, shotguns booming.

My father's shotgun is always to be treated with great respect. The long double-barrelled relic, with its beautiful curved hammers and balanced heft in the hand, must be broken open and the shells inserted directly into the breech, each shell connected to a separate trigger. You must always be prepared, always know where the gun is pointing. If you pull both triggers at once, the kick drives the stock deep into your shoulder, and if you're a young boy looking for something to shoot and the gun accidentally goes off – *boom boom!* – and blows up the dirt at your feet, the kick will rip through you and knock you down. And all the crows in the high trees will laugh at you, once, as they vanish, not to be seen for hours.

My uncle's gun is shorter, modern, a pump-action thrill you feed with shells on its underside and then lift easily into the air to fire and pump, fire and pump, as the squawking birds try to peel back into the sky. Uncle's gun slides more easily up to its target, and its shine reflects the duller patina on my father's gun. But the main difference between hunters is in the eye and arm, and it's my father who bags more birds, his arm the stronger, the steadier, as its extension sweeps the sky and pulls down bird after bird in its sudden-death blasts.

My uncle doesn't mind that he's tallied fewer ducks.

He doesn't even mind getting no birds at all. From what he tells us over supper, I know he likes waiting in the reeds, waiting for the good luck that might be heading his way – perhaps the birds will come close – likes letting the first ones go by, tiny teals with their whistling wings, waiting, holding back the urge to jump up and fire. If he waits for my father's signal – the pulling back of the hammers – if he holds down his hound-dog blood that wants only to leap and pull and pump before the birds are even close enough to hit, much less kill, if he waits, then he's rewarded by the perfect moment: standing and raising his gun and with minimal sighting firing into the breast of the great green-headed mallard only now aware that a man is in the sloughs.

But the real joy for Uncle is getting away from the city, eating my mum's homemade cooking, and drinking. My parents worry about him: he isn't looking after himself, he's drinking too much. He starts as soon as he arrives, which makes me think he's started already. But there's never any wobbly walking with Uncle, he's a big man and never stumbles, never misses on the steps upstairs to the cool bedrooms. He sets them up for my mother and father when he's barely in the door, although my mother never drinks, so he has to drink hers, too. Sitting around the kitchen table telling stories, he and my father toast and smile and toss back little glasses of golden fluid.

We're happy this time he's brought his wild son with him, only thirteen and already in trouble with the cops, his too-handsome wavy hair making everyone dare him into greater feats of adolescent bravado. I'm not told the details, but I'm not asked to leave the table either. What needs to be said beyond the ears of the youngest will be said elsewhere, on the hunt itself, or when I'm in bed. I know the son is unpredictable, and yet we're glad he's here. From what my father has said before, I know we must keep the son away from the guns, he's fast and foolish, he's too young. It's my older brother's job to handle him, and we leave them to it, watching only now and then as they drive back and forth into town, since nothing here on the farm holds the city cousin's interest for long.

When the hunt is over and the meals have been eaten and the drinks drunk, it's time to climb into the big Buick and drive back to the city. It's a long three hours to keep the alcohol from slipping up to Uncle's eyes and pulling down the lids. My father hasn't tried to stop Uncle from drinking, he's given up, but he does ask him not to leave until morning, when he's – what's the word my father uses: better? fresher? My mother puts coffee in his Thermos and homemade buns in his bag. The sky is darkening, the early darkening of autumn, when the two of them, fat uncle and our wild cousin, drive off.

We speculate about how far Uncle will get before he decides he can't drive all the way: maybe to town, maybe only to the Angle Bridge, certainly not as far as the first blacktop highway. We know what happens then: he climbs heavily into the back seat to sleep it off, and his son takes over.

My whole family seems to want just to stand outside

after our visitors have left us to the farm again. We're all bothered about that crazy boy driving those fast high-ways, bothered and a bit envious, Uncle in the back beyond worry or question. We wait for Mum or Dad to make the first move, for only one of them can lead us back to ourselves.

No one is much in love with the army in our family. Relatives of our grandparents had been in the Prussian army in the nineteenth century, and I've seen old photographs of proud stiff men with pencil-thin moustaches posing in military uniforms. These men seem incapable of laughter. Occasionally their wives pose with them, in a different setting, and they too seem scarcely to have felt the lift of love in their hearts. Of course, such photos are the style of the times; not for them the silly, unseemly horsing around of their later Canadian offspring, who inherit their future.

With such rigour in our family backbone, our pioneer grandparents are ready for anything – and much that they're not ready for comes to them as well: the Great War, and then the next war, too, both against the mother country they left. There's confusion and conflict; the old people still speak in German and don't feel right as the trains full of troops go by.

Why my uncle signs up is no longer clear. He's heading overseas during the Second War, then he runs away, to my mother – his sister – for help. He begs her to hide him from the military police. He says he can't go over there and shoot at his cousins (he calls them cousins although he's never met them). Does my uncle use this argument to work the heartstrings of my mother when really he simply couldn't face what was coming? Is he afraid of crossing that ocean, of shooting and getting shot at? Who wouldn't be? But he's also a happy man who loves dancing and women and drinking, a life of sport inside his body that keeps wanting always to get out through some avenue not made by a German bullet.

Once he hides in our house, once in the barn. Both times he's unable to escape the net of the military police. I'm born after this adventure has unfolded, but I still feel some of my uncle's resignation because it has entered the mist that hangs over the family. To join the army in the first place is a kind of betrayal, giving in to what this place calls for in the face of a longer call. And yet joining up is a way out of poverty and not knowing. He makes a choice, then regrets it, changing his mind as the door closes. Then comes the second betrayal: he cannot fight for his country right now, yet nevertheless he's not quite a traitor and a coward. The issues seem too complex for such straightforward terms and for a boy to whom war is a solitary game played atop a snowbank.

In his place, what would I do? Would I kiss my mother and father and march off in my woollen uniform and heavy boots to join the great debacle? Would I dodge beforehand or go AWOL when I realize I'm not cut out for such work, assuming I'm clear-headed enough to understand where the world and I meet and disagree?

Would I lie in my bunk and smoke Player's endlessly, enjoying their availability, and think about the women who love me when I dance with them at the canteen? I'm making the reverse journey of my parents, back to the rotten old womb of Europe where they were peasants, where fathers fought and died in the Franco-Prussian War and where their ancestors lived in forests and hills.

At least no one calls me Kraut. I would swing my fists then, defend my honour even if it means I take a beating, my face swollen afterwards as I lie on the blankets looking at the bunk above me, some old German nursery song passing through my head.

❖

Our neighbours the Juskowiaks come from a faraway land and have about them an air of mystery and good will. They're both, it seems, happy to be here, in this country, especially this part of the country, where few bother them. Talking with my parents, they break into smiles, and their language tumbles out of them, a language that sets them apart. I can't understand what they're saying. My parents listen carefully, my mother replying in German, my father nodding but speaking English in his turn. I'm content to listen as one might listen to unfamiliar music.

Their house is small, its walls covered with pale blue plaster, the roof thick as a thatch. I've never seen a house like it. This is the kind of home you'd find in a foreign land or a fairy tale, one with a sad ending for the children who have wandered away from their parents. I want to go inside, but because it's only mid-morning we are not invited in for coffee but expected instead to continue on to town. Standing around gives me time to see more.

The man is small, with tiny round wire glasses of a type I've not seen before, short blond hair, and thin lips. His round wife clutches to her apron two boys who seem willing to be gripped by their mother. The boys look up at the adults; they can understand what is being said and I cannot. When they first appeared at school, they were inseparable, and the teacher was concerned she'd have to put them in the same grade, they needed each other so. It didn't take long for the rest of us to learn they were German. But none of us teased them; something in their faces told us to hold our tongues. We didn't exactly pity these kids who dressed and talked funny, but we found it hard to reach out, afraid of what we might touch.

I learn from my mother that Heinz, the farmer across from this family, helped to bring them to Canada. Heinz has a big barn, a big house, two tractors, trees and lawn all around the house, and sections of cultivated land and pasture on which to raise cattle and make money. Once he helped set up the family on the farm across from his own, he more or less forgot them, seeing them maybe as a sign of the poverty he had managed to pull himself out of. Or perhaps he was simply too busy with his own life.

My older brother tells me later the stories that I could feel — some strangeness in the air — but not fully grasp.

He works with Mr. Juskowiak on and off during one season, cutting brush out of the ditches in a gang of men from the community, a crew mostly Ukrainian. During the lunch breaks my brother and the German find shade under the trees lining the ditch. They share meals, and the German speaks to my brother about his life before Canada, tales he wouldn't tell any other crew member because the war is still too near.

He'd been in the Hitler Youth, and he spoke about his first uniform, and the rows of blond boys marching. When he joined the army, he didn't know on which front he'd be fighting. Men left and didn't come back. The aerial bombing and the fear came later, his wife searching with other women for food in the rubble. They didn't know what would happen to them when they understood that Germany would lose the war. He told my brother about foreign soldiers in the street, lost and dead relatives, then the letter from Heinz, the long wait for paperwork, and the ship that carried them away.

My sister told me that he handed our dad a small black and white photograph he had taken, of bodies in a pile. She wasn't supposed to see the picture. She didn't tell me what it meant, and I didn't know.

This farmer's different from Heinz and my father and all the other farmers: his buildings small and rundown, his animals scrawny, his fields sandy and poor. While my father is relaxed around his animals, the German's bearing is stiff and wary. I'm old enough to recognize such difference but not yet able to see the history out of which it grows.

He is not a bitter man, but kind, his wife even kinder. When they see me in town, they urge their sticky home-made candy on me and talk to me in their strangled English. I am polite because I can feel something new about them, a giddy gratitude in their every act, from pulling up potatoes to feeding the pigs. I detect no envy towards the rich man Heinz across the road. They seem never to forget that once they had no food and no clothes except what they wore. Now they're free from such calamities, and their boys safely walk the half-mile to school.

Sometimes I walk with them, or rather, just ahead of them, covering the last sandy half-mile to the one-room school, listening to them jabbering behind me. I wonder what it would be like to have such a co-conspirator. I marvel at their short pants and their knobby knees and their big shoes. They have much to learn before they catch up to me, before they begin to be anywhere near as happy as their parents. They make me think my own mum and dad should be happier, and I wonder about all the things that happened to them – things I don't know about – while I thought all they were doing was looking after me.

❖

Naturally gregarious, my mother enjoys the company of my many uncles and aunts, some more than others, of course: coming from a family of fourteen kids you're bound to have favourites. More than the family tug-of-war, language holds them all together. When her siblings visit, she speaks her mother tongue. She's a different person in German, her speech rapid, suddenly removed from her children, who can't understand her. My mother and her skinny brother with his fat wife gabble, my aunt's English bearing an accent I can't always get beyond and which I never hear in my mother's voice. Mum loves not just these people but the chance to attune her ear and twist her tongue (or so it seems to me).

My mother's parents are so old they speak hardly at all – or at least not when I'm there, in the kitchen of their tiny old house in the city's north end, where they live with their unmarried oldest son, one of my mother's favourite brothers because he's chosen to look after them. When I do hear them talk, I wonder how they can tell what's being said, the words like bitten-off pieces of air hardened in their mouths. Mum sometimes speaks to my father in German, but he answers in English, unwilling, apparently, to join in.

After the relatives leave, driving back to their own farm, my mother moves with new animation on the way to her garden. She calls the dogs to go with her, takes a hoe in hand. On one side of the garden gate the long grass leans in from the bush, on the other side we cut the grass and call it lawn. Both places produce snakes foraging for mice or lying in the sun.

My mum sees the snake only as it twists away from her. She leaps and screams, full of real fright. This scream sends the dogs into the grass, their front legs bounding stiffly forward. One of them grabs the snake in his mouth, shakes it back and forth and throws it into the air, catches it and bites it again, throws it again while my mum runs for the garden and the safety of her rows of dirt. When the snake is dead, the dogs don't wolf it down in a gulp or two, as they do a fat harvest mouse, but leave it to shrivel in the sun. My father comes then with his pitchfork.

"They come out of nowhere," my mother says vehemently, then mutters: "I should never have been a farmer's wife."

My father laughs. "One day the dog's going to throw one right at you, and it'll catch around your ankle." My mother shudders.

I understand how she feels; her shudder races up my own spine, but it's not in me to scream. The sudden movement in the grass startles me, too, the snake frantic to get away.

What I want is my father's calmness, his savvy as he wields the pitchfork, its thick wooden handle shiny from use, the three tines gleaming silver. Wrapping a snake a foot and half long around those spikes and then pitching the mess into the farthest reaches of the grass where no one goes – now that's a skill I could use.

How does he decide which snake is worthwhile carrying back to the chickens, who peck its body so that it seems to jump and twist upward under their powerful jabs, everything else turned to dust and excrement by their scrabbling attention. Such mysteries are so natural to my father he can't conceive of teaching them to me. My mother's screaming, on the other hand, I might learn too easily, and I don't want to feel skilled in expressing fear so readily.

When my father teases my mother, my own developing brattiness is encouraged. He sets me free to imagine, briefly, how their lives must entangle. What I don't understand is why she married a farmer if she didn't want to be a farmer's wife. Weren't there other men to pick from? I know she worked for my dad's sister, helping in her house, and that my father came to visit and fell in love. For a woman who thinks and talks about the future more than the past, she must have been able to see where she would end up. Right here, with the snakes and the dogs and me.

❖

On Sunday morning my father takes us to the small church where we all sit on one pew, singing on cue from the minister. I know that my father believes what he hears and I want to share that faith, to be like him, but in my own youthful yearnings I can find no conviction so deeply felt.

I don't want to stop at Aunt Mabel and Uncle Bill's on the way home. Mum and Dad in the front seat are debating whether we should. Most Sundays we watch as their farm comes into sight and rolls past. The big barn announces itself sooner than the house, and I bet my dad is thinking about the muck ankle-deep in the corral. It's the house that causes us to turn in: its two stories seem blunted, and no grass or flowers add gracefulness to counter the bits and pieces of machine parts lying by the front step.

This Sunday my parents have been affected by the sermon, and so – also, perhaps, because my older brother (who would want to go straight home) is not with us – we pull in. A cowering dog greets us, its tail tucked deeply between its legs, its teeth showing in a dangerous smile. We knock on the broken screen door, and a long moment later, my mum pushes open the door and leans her head in.

"Hello, anybody home?" she calls, though she knows – we all know – Aunt Mabel's home. She's always home, held there by her physical weakness and her new baby. Sometimes one of Uncle Bill's sisters comes to help, but not this Sunday. When my aunt appears in the doorway between the kitchen and the living room, she's still in a housecoat although it's past noon. She hugs my mum and dad before returning her hands to the back of a chair for support. Happy to see someone, she is also embarrassed that she isn't prepared for visitors, and she's soon overtaken by her weariness.

The kitchen is cluttered with laundry, dishes stacked in the sink, a broom leaning against the cupboard as if just a moment ago someone had been busy.

"I can't keep up," she's saying.

"That doesn't matter," Mum replies, which surprises me. "You need to look after yourself and the baby first." She glances at the dishes in the sink as if she can hardly control herself from leaping up, unsure whether the good and right thing to do, the Christian thing, is to ignore them and focus on my aunt or wash them.

My dad leaves to find Uncle Bill in the yard. I know he'll be the same snuff-chewing, big-smiling, fat, joking man I've seen in town stumbling out of the beer parlour and into his truck when he should be home looking after his wife and child, or at least his cows. I don't blame him because he tries hard, always buying more land in the marsh for more hay, going to the auctions to get more machines and cattle, sure somehow he'll make the kind of money he wants.

What I don't understand is why he changed his name: he used to be Bill Schmidt and now he's Bill Smith. I guess he didn't want that rolling sound, although lots of people call him Schmidt anyway. When my mother's mad at him for not looking after his family, she calls him "that Bill Schmidt," spitting the word out in a way you can't spit out "Smith."

I sit on one of the hard kitchen chairs. My aunt does not invite us into the living room, which is tidy but not the place where you meet your guests. She struggles to make coffee. My grandmother adopted her into their family although when I ask, no one ever says why. I've heard she's the illegitimate daughter of one of my dad's older brothers – my dad's the fourth in a family of six brothers and two sisters – but I don't even bother trying to pry open that mystery. No one will tell me anything: whoever knows the truth will take it to the grave. I'm not sure I want to know anyway.

I'm picking at my Sunday pants, trying to be good while they're drinking coffee. Aunt Mabel offers me a cookie, one of those thin wafery store cookies with pink insides that come wrapped in crinkly clear cellophane. I've always wondered what they taste like – they look appealing – but when I bite into it, stale dryness fills my mouth. Even the pink sugar is tasteless. I wish my mother had brought along her raisin cookies. Uncle Bill may have more money and land than we do, but he has to eat these cookies.

I'm getting restless when a sound comes from the living room, a thin, mewling sound. My aunt goes into the room, my mother behind her. I follow them in. A crib is set up along one wall. Both women are bending over it. Here is the child that was born with something wrong, what my mother calls a blue baby. She's already had one operation on her heart and will need another. My aunt lifts her up. The child's face is dark. My mother turns to look for me. I know now why my aunt has no energy, all her worry pouring into such helpless imperfection.

On the way home, I sit in the back and watch the clouds out the rear window, my head tipped back. My mother's sister had a boy who couldn't move his legs and arms right, who was kept upstairs where his mother and older sister tended him lovingly. How they cried when he died! The coffin so small – that upset me, too.

My neck aches. I watch hydro poles go by. Sometimes the line branches off on a different road and I look out into space again, across fields with farmhouses tiny in the distance, sometimes surrounded by sheltering trees, sometimes huddled up against the barns. How does it happen that one child – me – is normal and another isn't? Is there something in us that makes us go wrong? I wonder if that's why Uncle Bill changed his name, to avoid something he knew was heading his way.

I think of my other Uncle Bill, my dad's oldest brother, born Wilhelm in Germany in another century. The month after I was born he died, as Bill Wilson. He changed his name to the most inconspicuous one he could imagine, unable to bear any longer his German heritage in this new world. My dad never spoke about the reasons. His older brothers are unknown to me, shadowy figures who spent time in the car factories of Detroit and sent home small, loving cards at Easter to their mother, their handwriting as strangely elaborate as hers.

I'm counting fence posts now. We're almost home, the gravel giving way to smoother clay. I promise myself I will never change my last name, no matter what. The teacher in Grade 1 took my first name away and made me Dale because there was another David in class, and she didn't like his second name – Martin – as much as mine. She thought I could be a better Dale than he could be a Martin.

I'm used to my new name now, kids at school calling me Dale although my parents still call me David. I'm not ashamed of going from David to Dale. It's not like changing your own name from Schmidt to Smith or even Wilhelm to Bill. There's no shame in what others do to you.

❖

My sister's driving back to the farm. I'm in the passenger seat. The humpy car is moving too fast around this corner, the only real corner on the five miles to town. The gravel on the curve acts like rollers, the back of the car suddenly trying to catch up to the front. She turns the wheel one way, then the other, as we slide off the road and into a shallow ditch. I leap from the car, crying loudly, run and half run the half-mile home, my sister pursuing me, hoping to make my father understand that what has happened is not so serious as my sobbing.

As I get older, I see how the west side of the road drops into the big ditch. I turn to watch the roll of gravel the grader leaves when it levels potholes, a roll that can catch a front tire and pull a car into the ditch. I think of Billy Turko, who didn't want to slow down for his corner – he'd been driving straight and fast from a dance in Plumas, and slowing down must have seemed an inconvenience he couldn't afford, seeing how late it was getting to be. He hit the corner too fast and must've caught the gravel. The car veered, slid, rolled. Billy flew out, and the car rolled once more, coming to rest atop him. He was only a few years ahead of me in school.

Then there's the Angle Bridge. Not straight, not built to minimize the span, it almost but not quite manages to keep the adjoining roads aligned. The road curves going

into and out of the bridge, and when you approach it
you have to remember its peculiarities. Sometimes we
stop on the bridge and look down, a little dizzied by the
depth of water coursing against the pilings. From the
other side of the bridge the water seems altered, thinned,
a slant of sun making it all surface and glitter.

Here we look for remnants of the bridge's latest
victim. If I could drive, if I were travelling late at night
on this unfamiliar road, eager to get home, would I hear
the gravel under my tires grow louder, telling me to slow
down? Would I be one of the ones who push harder,
hitting the bridge with too much speed, feeling the curve
only as I take out the railing and cascade with a metallic
*whumpph* into the dark water below?

When my sister marries, she's been living in the city
for several years, and the wedding and reception are held
there. We have a second dance back here, in the hall
where she'd been courted by local men. Our neighbours
and friends and their families, those from farms and those
in town, crowd into the hall where the Rossnagel boys
play their specialty of foxtrot and waltz on the accordion,
fiddle, banjo, and guitar. Guests arrive from out of town,
including an uncle, aunt, and two girl cousins, the
youngest two grades ahead of me.

Because she's nervous about the farm – the chicken
droppings, the snuffling dogs, the snakes on the lawn, the
outhouse – I'm eager to exploit my cousin's uneasiness.
Our families thrust us together, expecting us to play, but
I know she wants to escape to the older siblings who are
already allowed to drive off on their own. I get mad

when she won't listen to me. I push her into the big box of chicken feathers my mother's saving for pillows. The room explodes with white fluff, and my cousin emerges, wronged and sputtering, bawling for her mother.

Of course I am yelled at, but not so badly as I anticipate. Some of the wrath from my father and my uncle is drained off by their laughter at the sight of her, clothes and hair full of feathers. My aunt, on the other hand, sees the meanness in me, while my mother tries to show me how poorly I've acted and how compromised *she's* been. My uncle looks at me strangely, probably wondering, as I squint up at him, what it must be like to have a son, grateful perhaps he has only daughters. He's younger than my dad, the baby of his family, as I am of mine, and I think fondly of him, especially on the Victoria Day weekend when he brings fireworks from the city and sends them screaming up from the lawn, terrifying the dogs. My aunt enjoys these nighttime displays although she is herself a little nervous about the danger and often says: "Be careful, Ernie."

The night of my sister's second wedding celebration, the danger of alcohol presents itself to my aunt. We all know she's fearful of my uncle's drinking. At the dance he meets an old friend and is invited back to a house in town. I end up in a car with my cousin, waiting for him to come out. She and I are in the back seat.

"I don't think your dad's had very much to drink. He'll be okay."

"I hope so."

I know she's worried, but because I trust my family's judgment about my uncle, I'm free to make her worry more. I know my uncle will be fine, but she doesn't. I want to help her worry, to see what she'll do. Waiting in the driveway, I enjoy the broadening prospects of my meanness.

When my uncle returns, he's fine, he's happy. We drive through empty streets, slowly, and before we're out of sight of the last street light, I whisper to my cousin the two words that make her even more nervous: "Angle Bridge."

As we pass safely over its timbers, I feel as if I'm sharing her anxiety, forgetting I'm the one who put it there in the first place. I think my cousin understands this bit of theatre, the genius of the country child who's bored and performs a little villainy at the expense of the city cousin. I think she's enjoying this worry about her father's driving while full of whisky, as I am. I think she's playing her part well.

When we pull up into the yard behind several parked cars (one of them on the lawn), she surprises me. She leaps out of the car and bursts into tears. My aunt trundles down the porch steps to hold her. When my uncle comes around the front of the car, my aunt slaps his face and shouts: "Where have you been?" The glow from the yardlight makes us all yellow. My mouth is open, I'm trying to speak, but I don't know what to say. Nobody is looking at me anyway. My cousin and aunt retreat into the house. My uncle drifts after them. My mother leaves her hostess duties and finds me in the stairway.

"What happened?"

I present my uncle in a guiltless light. I explain that nothing happened, my cousin got upset about nothing.

She lets me go, and I have to find my cousin and explain to her that she didn't understand the game we were playing. But she's gone upstairs and she'll stay there, she and her mother, until the party ends.

In the morning they'll pack and leave early, and I'll have time to speak up then, if we're not all too stiff with one another. Maybe I'll tell her I'm sorry I upset her, I didn't mean any harm, I knew things would work out and thought she knew it, too.

Or maybe I'll not say anything but just smile and wave as they drive down the lane and start on the five miles to town.

❖

Red's my friend, sometimes my best friend, or at least the one who shares my circumstances: farm, church, school, and parents who often visit for winter meals, card games, and gossip. Sometimes in summer his dad loads us into the back of his two-ton truck and drives to a large shallow lake with sandy beaches surrounded by willows and marsh. We cannot imagine the length of the water snakes until someone finds one and holds it by its tail, its head jiggling near the water. We love the stones and the muck a little farther out and at last the hard sand underfoot even as the water bobs up to our chins.

Red is more daring than I, plus he can swim – or at least he can move through the water and stay out where it's over his head, feeling with his toes for a sandbar. He often wrenches the inner tube away from his sisters, then

floats out as far as he can before his parents holler at him
to come back in. He's reckless, but his father keeps him
in line.

Red's always experimenting – with a chemistry kit, a
wood-burning kit, a BB gun. He's got gadgets and in the
living room a whole row of encyclopedias he likes to
browse through. His ideas of what the world is like and
how he's going to fit in seem without much basis to me.
But he's Red, and not to be contradicted; he'll turn on
you, tease and test you, and show you up for a dolt. We
move beyond waving guns and sticks in the imaginary
faces of bandits and troublemakers, and start waving
them at each other, especially when I'm irritated with
his relentless jabs aimed at making me mad because I've
thwarted a suggestion that was silly or dangerous or fun
only for him.

The night I sleep over, I'm required to sleep in his
bed. His parents stay in town longer than mine, and I
want to keep playing that night and the next day, thinking that everything ahead will be more of the same:
more fun. There's no place else to sleep but with Red.
His family is big, and all the beds are taken by sisters.

In the bed it dawns on me: this isn't my bed, with its
own comfort, familiarity, and smell. Red's in here as well.
The bed's full of crumbs, and sand, some grains close to
small stones. Red falls asleep and begins to snore and
then thrash around, murmuring half-things I half hear. I
realize I may never get to sleep. The house is dark and
the night outside darker, nothing's alive except Red and
me, and he's in another world, rolling and pushing against

me, making me push back, which does little good. Eventually, he's pushing so hard I'm propping an arm against the wall. I think about going to the other side of the bed and starting again, but such a step would mean I'd have a story next morning, and it's a story I don't want to tell.

The night air smells of hay. Before dawn, still clinging to the edge of the bed, I make comparisons. I'm better at track than Red, who can't run or catch well. He's quicker in science class, his eyes ablaze with the problems he's expected to grasp and go beyond. But when dawn finally arrives, I see him in the fetal position we all, I've learned, get back to in the night. And I realize I have no idea about his dreams and his secret life, how much lust may be in him for girls. I'm feeling stirrings and confusions, but not as much as some boys. Red seems to avoid the subject entirely, postponing it until he's sure about . . . what, I don't know.

Without waiting for breakfast I dress and pedal the gravel road home, my bicycle tire pushing into sand. The house and poplars signal from the turn, where my neighbour sometimes drops me off after school and drives on with her kids, leaving me always a little surprised that I still have that half-mile to go. By the time I get home this morning, it's hard to believe our place has not changed; it feels as if I've been on a long journey, that our house should have aged and the season changed, that it wasn't just the night before that I last saw my mother and father drive away but a whole lifetime ago.

This is the year I start writing things down, more than

required by school. Not quite jottings or lists, maybe a turn of phrase, a word picture that passes through my thinking in such a way that I'm compelled to see what it looks like on paper.

One evening Red and I find ourselves outside with time on our hands before our parents finish visiting. We gather twigs and leaves, because fire is in our minds. We're old enough, and Red has matches, though only three. I trust his plan, but after the first match only a leaf has been scorched. His idea to make the twigs smaller is a good one, and I go with it, and watch him fail again.

One match left. That's when I give him my scrap of paper. I realize I'm burning my first poem, and I savour the significance, hoping it will help those twigs into flames we can hold our hands out to. We feed twigs into the fire, then bigger twigs, and the snow melts slowly back in an expanding circle.

Only when we stomp out the flames and notice that darkness has set in do I suddenly miss that paper. On the way home, sleepy in the back seat, away from Red and his sudden schemes, I try to remember exactly what I'd written there.

# — THE BOUNDARIES —

My father is often cold and wears more clothes than any man I know. Only in high summer does he open the top three buttons on his shirt, where white skin contrasts deeply with his sunburned neck and face. When one of my brothers drives the tractor – in high gear – in from the west field, he stands, his shirt flapping in one of the sure signs of summer. My father never gets this loose. At one time he must have been as tough and wiry as his sons, and in old photos, when he was their age, he stands erect. But I don't get to see this younger man my brothers must have known. Even in July my father's body never forgets working outside in minus-30 weather, wearing wool mitts inside leather mitts, lined caps with lugs large enough to cover his big ears, and, always, his long underwear.

Now it's autumn: there's time in the day to spare – no seeding, no haying, no harvesting left, deer hunting

not yet begun, the feel of winter only mildly in the air
– and a neighbour is having a birthday party. Other kids
will be there, I don't know who; maybe just little ones.
I can't decide about going. At home I'd be with my
brother, who is no fun any more, so I go along, hoping
for the best.

The neighbour's house is made of faded yellow brick.
The machines from the field have been pulled right up
to the house. The dog's always growling and raising the
tangled hair on its neck. None of the kids is my age. I
manage to keep myself amused by sometimes running
outside with them and sometimes staying in where the
adults all talk at once, excited about this unusual party.
They act as if I'm not there, which means they might say
or do something I shouldn't witness, which makes me
want to stay. Then they realize I *am* there and scold me
for snooping.

The seven other couples are not interested in me.
They're younger than my parents; hence the little kids.
They've organized a game around the husbands' feet.
The men sit in a row in the living room, sheepishly
removing shoes and socks. I'm not surprised when it
becomes evident that my dad is the only man in long
underwear, which shows below the cuffs of his pants. Its
natural beige announces that he needs more warmth
than his younger neighbours, who haven't learned yet
how fast the cold can come.

I wear long underwear myself. Later, in high school, I
see that the most adventurous young men do not. In fact,

they love to brag about the cold, not even wearing boots, sliding along the icy white tire tracks on leather-soled shoes. They point to the bottom of the pant legs of those of us who wear long underwear. But they ride the bus home or live in town. Others of us arrive home on iffy roads, and have to walk in the cold and storms, and only long underwear stops the wind that cuts through our pants. Because I don't want to be seen as a chicken, I compromise, cutting off the underwear at calf length so it never appears in public bunched up under bulky socks. I can show my naked ankles, stick my bare legs out from under my desk – join the ranks of the tough kids – without having to be completely reckless.

When the wind finds my unprotected ankles, how-ever, it bites deeply. I'm walking home from the half-mile turn, and I hear my father say, "You've wrecked a good thing," when he finds I've cut the ends off the legs. He won't bother himself to understand my need for the right look. This desire to belong he might not have felt in his own time. He was, after all, thirteen when the First World War broke out, forced to live on what the family grew and on their own strength, on their prayers and sweat, his father and oldest brother interned for part of the winter in a camp for German aliens. He might not know about looking good in someone else's eyes.

A blindfolded wife is led into the living room, where she kneels to fondle the naked feet of the men. She tries to identify her husband's feet by feel alone. The women laugh and squeal, the men groan. My father sits at the beginning of the row, so the first woman will feel his feet first. I don't want a strange woman to take my father's feet in her hands, searching the knobby toes for clues. If she gets to his ankle, she'll find his underwear and know to move on to the next pair of feet. My dad's laughing uncomfortably now.

I hide in the bathroom. We have only a sink at home, for draining away the wash water into the bush behind the house, creating a wet area with long grass between house and garden. We use a tin tub for bathing. This house is more modern, the people more up to date. In here, a tub has been built in and the sink is attached to the wall. The colour matches that of the toilet, which I sit on to admire this green I've never seen before. It's not grass green, nor the deep green of a male mallard's head, but a green suffused with a bluish tint that holds my eye. I feel closer to this colour than I do to the adults in the other room or to the kids running past the closed door.

I don't want to go back out there. How can my dad let himself be humiliated in front of those people? They're supposed to be his friends, but I guess because they live in a newer world than ours they get to laugh at everything that's not like them.

❖

Girls are still off limits; I can't figure out how to approach them. I know girls in the grades above and below, and in a few years I'll be holding them during fall dances at school. Eventually, I know, everything that has to happen will happen. I know the road ahead: girls, women, marriage. What I can't see yet is the particulars.

So it's a boy's world, and Wiener and I have a pact: to show each other our penises. We don't call them penises because we haven't much use for the word. Wiener's a town kid, bigger than me, with something special about him, something strange about his penis, hence his nickname. I can't imagine it. I'm frustrated by my lack of knowledge; I want to see why Wiener's penis has made him Wiener.

I haven't seen anyone else's — there's a problem with vocabulary — thing, cock, prick, bone. I have some knowledge of sex. Our school tries, but the older boys laugh and guffaw while we younger ones laugh uncomfortably at the statue with the erection in the guidance class film. I take my cue from the teacher, who's blushing and standing off to the side.

Perhaps my mother has taken me aside; I don't remember. Perhaps I was too embarrassed and stopped hearing. Certainly my father says nothing, assuming I should understand simply by seeing the animals on the farm. My father and brothers are modest, not given to boasting or un-shy displays. I'm on my own with glimpses at the urinals, when the bigger boys are a little cavalier with their zippers. Or at the wedding dances at the hall, when some drunk wanders out back and sprays the tree I happen to be passing.

After enough skinny dips in the dugouts and lakes, after joining the wider club that all older boys — boys becoming men — belong to, I lose interest, outgrow this fascination. As a doctor later says during a high school examination at which I'm required to strip, bend, and cough: "It's like a spark plug to a mechanic."

In the meantime, Wiener and his folks drive in from town. There's a meal my mother has worked hard to get right, for these people have money and therefore some clout. Mum likes company and likes to make the food and atmosphere just right. After the meal Wiener and I go outside, and that's where the bargaining begins.

"You go first," he says.

"No, you first."

He's bigger than me, taller. I can see he's not going to open up before I do. If my curiosity is to be sated, I will have to undo my buttons first.

And so I do. For a moment there it is, my tube, worm, thing, out in the air. There's a pause as we both look at it, me bending back on my heels, Wiener twisting away. Then he laughs and turns for the house. I run after him, fumbling with my buttons, but I know he's not going to keep his end of the bargain. I've been betrayed, and tears of rage spurt from my eyes. I bring down my fists on his back before he leaps up the stairs and into the kitchen where our parents rise to their feet. Wiener's mother is indignant, not interested in finding out the cause of this outburst but convinced that her child – her only child – is in the right and that I'm a brutish farm boy.

My own mother is embarrassed that I can't control myself when she has company – and of course I can't tell her what prompted my outburst – while the fathers sit down again, exchanging stories from their youths. I'm told to go outside on my own while Wiener stays in, under his mother's protection.

For days I plot my revenge, tell myself ways to humiliate Wiener, but nothing seems workable. I burn inside that I've been so gullible. I understand now what the word means – gullible – and my face hardens around the eyes and mouth. We cross paths at school, but neither of us says a word, locked into my humiliation, his triumph.

By the end of the week, walking home from school, it strikes me that nothing has changed. I've been duped, betrayed, humiliated. But I still have my good name, and he still has his stupid one.

❖

At the summer picnic I like to watch the men lob the heavy iron horseshoes. My father is good at making the spike sing, cigarette clamped in his jaw as his long throw goes curving down into the sand, where the shoe grabs and rings.

Others at the picnic are worth watching, too. Alvin swings the bat and drives the ball foul into the crowd. The ball travels so fast no one sees it; suddenly a boy crumples to the ground, gripping his leg and crying, screaming. He was too close to third base, everyone sees that now. We gather round, and someone says, "It's broken." His father comes running. Another man is already trying to unfold the boy. Smaller boys are shouting "Broken! Broken!" out across the field, their voices piercing as a killdeer's shriek.

Alvin sets the tip of his bat down on home plate and waits. He makes no gesture towards the boy. His stance tells us he will be patient. He can feel the power in his shoulders, and he's going to catch a good one off this pitcher and drive it straight. He has a reputation.

Delbert, the catcher on the other team, is not yet as good as his willingness to shove around the batters might suggest. He dives into the sand too much, and the way he holds his mitt shows that he's still half afraid of the ball. He seems to think risking injury is more important than winning. It's the last inning, his team's losing badly, but he still pretends he's going to win, running madly to catch the foul pop-ups. He yells, he kicks, he throws his mitt down. This is a man who shoots crows, takes their legs into the municipal office to redeem them for ten cents a pair. He scares the young women, who look at him with disgust and scream if he grabs for them.

When the game is over, Delbert leads Lady, his big Arabian, out of the little red barn. She tosses her head, and her long legs dance around before he mounts her and rides out of the schoolyard with a clatter, leaving hard marks in the packed sand. He leaves the circle the rest of us make. He ends up dead in Montana of a gunshot wound, before or after he broke the bank at one of the western circuses. His body comes all the way back. His mother puts him in the ground, in a sandy patch near others with his last name. We're quietly proud of him for being the wildest, for flinging himself through sheer hellish energy all the way into another country and death.

Jimmy is one of the poor kids. We are all poor kids,

none with much change except enough for one of the good, greasy hot dogs from the booth where women also prepare scoops of ice cream and slices of cold water-melon. But Jimmy and his sister are poorer. They once loaded a horse cart full of hazelnuts and tried to peddle them in town – for a joke, they said when few bought, but cash was entirely the point. Jimmy runs at the picnics, his blond hair flapping, for the cash.

Our races reward winners with up to twenty dollars for first prize. My father is one of the judges – someone recognized as scrupulous – and while he might have favourites, he certainly wouldn't allow any tug of the heart to enter into his decision-making when two runners cross the line together. Such a judge has to have not only a firm centre but a good eye. I'm proud of my father's ease among men, the respect they grant him, the cash he gives to the beaming, gasping winners.

Jimmy isn't without competition. Every young buck wants not just the money but the admiring glances of a girl he's sure he can work on later in the evening with a beer from the trunk of his car – running his hands up her arm and into her blouse before they find themselves eager for the slanted expanse of the back seat or, if the weather's right and not too damp, the bare ground, soft-ened by buttercups and cowslips and pussytoes, and in the air the sharp song of the whippoorwill.

Jordie is fast, and my brother is fast, but they enter the race more to feel the wind from Jimmy's heels than to win. Jordie can run, but his short body seems to struggle through the air as if it were water. When the Indians show up in their old cars, there's a silent one among them who can be a threat. At first the runners are a clump of bodies. Then, over the first few yards, Jimmy emerges out of the pack and stays there, lengthening the lead bit by bit. He seems not to be trying, just moving his legs, as if this is the way legs are meant to move. The others strain terribly, realization dawning again that the best they can do is second place or third.

At the finish where we have clustered, no envy or anger colours the faces. Everyone likes Jimmy, who's neither boastful nor falsely modest. We respect not just his speed but the way he takes success: not as his due but graciously, modestly, aware of himself. He's the son in a family that knows how to dodge that martyred look. We'd be unhappy if he didn't win the race, taking the twenty home, back to the farm he's not going to stay with, neither he nor his sister, his mother long dead, the father hardly ever coming into town.

By the time we drive home, I'm tired. Mum and Dad are tired, too, but their languor is less the effect of heat and wind and excitement than the afterglow of happy sociability. All day they talked with others, exchanging news about grain and government, eggs and people. They have stories to mull over for a week. The stories I'm living inside are different from theirs. Everything is settled for them: they live here, always will, knowing the same people, doing the same things. Sometimes – today – that seems lucky.

The high school dance is coming to a close. We've had our fun, dancing with one another, not noticing too much the tension in the air. Lots of people here are older than school age because the dance has been well advertised, and everyone likes the music. A skinny guy on saxophone gets us hopping, and the drums and double guitar rely on rock and roll tunes from Chad Allan and the Expressions. We've twisted and jived, foxtrotted. The summer heat wafts into the long hall, and we take off sweaters and jackets and watch the girls get down to bare shoulders and arms. The dance has been a success I've helped organize, getting the band and selling the tickets. We've made enough money to maybe have another dance later in the fall. Even guys who don't dance have enjoyed the evening, standing around at the back and goading one another to cross the floor and ask one of the girls. The girls have less shyness, some of them coming up to the boys and dragging them out. Or they dance with one another, turning on the smooth floor and dipping their joined hands up and down.

The last dance changes all this. This is when the pairing happens. Suddenly they're not boys and girls any more but men and women with longings that need to be expressed. What do you do when you're half aroused and terrified? You join the watchers, guys mostly though some girls, too, twin groups who look warily across the crowded dance floor at each other. The guys are afraid of being turned down – such a public embarrassment happens often enough. The girls will not cross the floor at the last dance to grab up a blushing young fellow. The last dance is the last chance for the couplings, the who with whom.

I watch my friend dancing with a young woman he's not danced with all night. He's said publicly (in the men's toilet) that she wasn't pretty enough to look at, and now he's waltzing with her, moving past the rest of us. His fingers point down her back in a V, meaning she's said yes, he can take her home after the dance.

My friend, whom I call the Stud, reaches heights of bravado I can only contemplate. He's been dancing with women all night, but mostly with one he particularly likes. But she's too young to go home with someone like him. She doesn't call him the Stud, of course, but maybe her mother does. I call him that only in my mind because he might pop me one in the mouth. He's got it all: looks, good hair, full lips, sweet smile, the status as a clever guy bound for a good job, skilled at track and field. He's not old enough to drive, but he's already lost his virginity to some girl from the town by the lake. Since then he never fails to give us the picture of his conquests. Sex for him is just the necessary outcome of being male.

The rest of us envy him his stature, the unconscious assumptions he makes about himself and everyone else. He's superior in many ways, although our envy doesn't compel us into the sexual field very far, not yet anyway. The older guys can better him from time to time, but he's accepted by them. The rest of us, the younger ones, sit it out for now, thinking mainly about getting out of town and into the city, where surely something better will happen.

When the Stud's in the pool hall, he's someone to notice. Of course, he wields his cue with the best of the older men, some wanting to pair up with him in doubles. It's during these games that one of the older men wanders over to him, the kind of guy who's always smiling and telling a funny story, everyone's pal. Without warning, he squeezes the Stud's penis. The Stud folds up at the waist and jerks away, and I can feel my own loins contract. When the others see, they laugh. The Stud blushes good-naturedly at this coronation, while the old man chuckles and talks about good German sausage.

Because the girl the Stud likes can't go home with him, he's got a choice: go home alone, or go with the girl anyone can go with. She's heavy and not attractive, but she's bright, and she talks easily and comfortably about how things feel. She and I work on the yearbook, and I think of her as a friend. She's funny and normal when we're trying to arrange the pages, but I know she's taboo. She's never going to make the top grades, never going to be in that group of girls who wear tight sweaters and win the hearts of guys from the city with cars and jobs and time enough to drink beer all weekend and drive them around, planted so close it's sometimes hard to see there are two people in the front seat. She's not going to make it into that picture, and she knows it, but she's got something she can do.

The Stud dances the last dance with her, sheepish grin on his face. She's beaming, dancing with the best boy in the school, as if she's snagged him and this is their wedding night. Maybe she has to think this way. Monday morning back at school my friend tells me the details. I'm not the only one he tells because I see now – if I haven't understood before – that telling the guys at the break behind the school when they're sneaking a smoke is part of the ritual. He says how easy she was to fuck, how eager to lift her skirt, how wet and ready she was, "like a pail of water," he says, dismissing her.

But that's not the end of it. My friend can drive, but he's too young to have a licence. He often gets rides; others are happy to drive him around. One guy in particular is willing to oblige, and I call him the chauffeur, a moody German guy who has finished Grade 12 but hasn't yet decided what he's going to do, sometimes working and sometimes not. He drives the Stud and the girl to her home, parks in the long driveway far enough from the house not to attract attention. He leaves them in the back seat where they've been making sucking noises and goes for a walk in the dark, for a piss and a smoke, waiting for them to be done and for the Stud to walk the girl up to the house.

He's standing in the moonlight when the Stud comes and says it's his turn, she's agreed that he, too, can have a go. He can't believe the Stud has talked her into such a deal; but the Stud is only covering his tracks. He didn't use a safe, and if she gets pregnant he doesn't want her to point the finger at him. He tells us his rationale behind the school. We can all picture the trembling German, sliding into the back seat and the arms of the girl. We can't help but admire the Stud's silver tongue in getting her to agree, seducing her twice in the same

night, pleading the chauffeur's case so ardently, so elo-
quently, that she succumbs again. My friend explains that
the German couldn't believe his luck, getting laid like
that when he's one of the gloomy guys girls don't nor-
mally look at.

It's hard to work with her after that. She knows he
told everyone, that's the way it works, and she wouldn't
want it any other way. She needs the glory of her own
conquest, if that's what it is, and she's willing, apparently, to be humiliated, to risk being labelled a whore,
not just loose.

But where is the tenderness in all this? I've seen tenderness between people, even if it's sometimes awkward
and strained. Now she's shy around me in a way that dis-
turbs me. After a while I begin to understand the lengths
to which she'll go to insert herself into the fabric of the
school. This desperation makes me sad, but it's something I also admire, for I can't imagine the depths of
desire in her, desire for acceptance and love and for self-
abasement and for men.

❖

The storekeeper is fat, his wife thin; their younger son
is mean to them, ignores them, smokes, drinks, drives
without a licence, drives too fast, combs his hair into an
extravagant wave, and gets a girl from the next town
pregnant. In this son's face you see scorn and loathing,
the rebelliousness that makes him disobey his father and
mother, and the handsomeness that helps him get away

with it. As if he likes being the horror of the town, or as if it hasn't yet occurred to him that he is.

It's a wonder his parents let him stay at home, don't hurl him into the street and curse him. They have compassion, especially the father, because the son is built like him: tough and muscular. The father knows too well and cannot bear the future that awaits this son, cannot stem his pity from flowing to his younger child. So nothing is done. His son's few friends gather around to worship him and emulate the wave in his hair and the insolence in his mouth, exactly what the young women at the dances seem unable to resist.

The older brother resembles their mother and is the mother's favourite. This brother stopped growing one day when he was twelve, and now he uses this quality of shortness to his advantage. He wins the long jump, flying high over the sand with his thin legs and baggy shorts, then strutting back to the judges for his ribbon. He has his mother's gift of gab, and in the school play he commands the stage easily, throwing out his voice to the back of the auditorium and finding feeling in lines that the director – the school's only English teacher, and she is half in love with him – hasn't until then noticed. He excels in the zone competition, goes to the provincials, wins. His mother in the front row stands and applauds when he accepts the trophy as best actor. The next day the town streams through the store to admire the gleaming tall silver trophy on the shelf above the ice cream freezer where the black and white television used to be.

Late in the afternoon he makes an appearance, coming into the store from the rooms in back.

My father never speaks about these young men, but I know what he thinks. He worries the younger, wild one will lead me and others into despicable acts. If we follow this bad example, we'll dishonour our family name; worse, we'll have to live with disgrace eating away at us until we take to drink and give up working hard, saving money, raising a family like the one he was raised in even though such a family is no longer possible, and he knows it.

He admires the older son, sees him as the one to follow if a model is required. My father appreciates achievement and confidence. But he worries about confidence becoming arrogance, even disrespect. He doesn't like the older son's lack of humility. He doesn't trust pride to last a lifetime. He doesn't want his own sons to build on a basis so personal, so fragile.

Because my father doesn't talk much, I've learned to watch carefully, to read his silences, the shapes of his mouth, his gestures, the way he allows my mother to speak (and speak and speak, sometimes, talking for both of them, or talking into the void that his wordlessness makes). I know my father not because of what he tells me but because a current of blood flows between us through our fifteen years. Does he know I judge his reticence – even when I agree with his assessments? My life with him can be that confusing, and the confusion can seem that necessary.

Yet for all that, my father supports the father of these sons, perhaps because he understands the difficulties the man is facing. His compassion rises. My father thinks the sons are taking advantage of their father, and his loyalty lies with the man. The sons should be the ones to change. He doesn't blame the father for being unable to bring up the sons to "honour thy father." He doesn't see that it's precisely this adult world joining together against the young that has brought the younger son to rebellion.

❖

The first neighbours to sell their farm and leave forever are John and Julia. Their only child, Walter, has already moved to Ontario, a job in a jam factory – now he has a wife and children. Julia used to pick my mother up on her way to town. My mother doesn't say so, but I know she's thinking Julia deserves more than that tiny whitewashed log house chinked with mud and manure – and so close to the ground, without any raised barrier to keep out frost and mice. When I drop over to pick up a basket of wild blueberries Julia's picked, I see her small kitchen, its sloped roof, the living room with its one picture – of Walter and his family. In this tiny house, upstairs (where she and John sleep) is only a few steps away.

I've seen the way John treats his white horses, Prince and Dan. In a temper, he'll lash out at them and make them start and pull against the harness, and then yell at them to stand still. His face is dark and gaunt, his baggy overalls never indicating what his body looks like. When he joins the dozen other men around the oval table at threshing time, his is the thickest accent and the strongest complaint. But now he's leaving all this behind. The cattle, the farm implements, the hoes and rakes, the dishes, the pails – all are being sold at auction. One day a crowd tramples the flowers, and the next day John and Julia drive away.

Then the man arrives who has bought their farm, which butts up against ours. Except I never see him: he's a hermit. I'm busy with school, trying to understand what I want to do. But I hear rumours. The hermit doesn't actually live in the house. Apparently a neighbour drove in and saw that he had made a corner of the granary into a makeshift home. The granary was newer than the house, off the ground; maybe that was the attraction. The neighbour said there was hay in one corner where somebody obviously slept. Apparently he had enough money to buy the farm but not enough for a bed – or a chair, table, or anything else.

I know about eccentrics: the man who lives in a house on a pile of sand, the place poorly lit, the dog on the couch his only company while his wife lives down the road and throws garbage and eggshells out the kitchen door – which means she stinks all the time and yet refuses to eat sandwiches made by any hand other than her own at summer picnics. That's eccentric. A man who doesn't sleep in his own house is strange.

The story ends with his suicide, winter almost over. "One night too many alone," says a kid in my class who pretends he knows such things because that's the way he thinks the girls will pay attention. Someone must have called the police, and the cop came by and found him. Or maybe it was the neighbour who blundered on the body, hanging or shot, I don't know. I might have been at the reach of our property that day, walking the fenceline. I might have been looking at his place while he was dying.

What did he think at the end when he looked out that granary door into the snow and white light? What did he flee from that was so bad he had to live and die this way? John and Julia fled to somewhere presumably better. Maybe the suicide felt he was doing the same thing.

When it's my turn to leave – after high school – what will I feel? Is it true that men without women go crazy? John could not have survived without Julia, I'm sure. My father wouldn't think of living without my mother. It would be against his religious beliefs and his better judgment. He married late in life, and he understands the need for a wife.

My neighbour stands as an example of what can happen if a man isn't careful. He wasn't the kind of man whose life was full enough with the farm and animals and the evenings of throwing his clothes down and leaving them there. He might not have been that self-contained, even before he made that crazy decision to run away to a new life in a granary. I want to make sure I get connected in a way he wasn't. I'd like to skip right out of this life and get to the part where I'm no longer this self, yet still me – settled, but with the future ahead of me. I'm not going to be like the man who ran away, who came here and died, I know; but just how I'll be different is what worries me.

◆

Sherri's need for me – for something – is so strong it scares me. A friend drives the two of us to her home after the dance, a ten-minute ride. I put my arm around her skinny shoulders, and she snuggles into me. The three of us are talking about the dance, the music, whether the next dance will be longer. It's already past two, and we've left the lights of the town behind. Only the beams of our car lights bounce off the gravel road.

What we don't talk about is Sherri's parents, how they're different from everyone else's, how her mother's sister is also part of the family, having produced a child by her brother-in-law, Sherri's father. No one speaks about this, yet we all seem to know what goes on in that household. Who wouldn't want to know how such a system works? Does he sleep with the women on alternate nights, or week on, week off? What does the woman not in favour think about her sister? Is she angry, or relieved, or indifferent entirely, used to the arrangement? Or are they ever together, all three in a bed? Or was it just one night that he slipped into his sister-in-law's room? What happened then: what screaming, what deals leading to what arrangements?

I want to ask Sherri what she thinks, but how can I phrase it: *How do you feel about your dad and your aunt?* Something vague and open-ended like that, to which she'll look up at me, shocked, and say: "What do you mean?" She'll deny it, of course, even though her aunt isn't afraid to show up pregnant in town, and the kid looks just like the father. Yet they haven't been drummed out of town; only a few mothers click their tongues when they pass by. Everyone learns to live with this oddity.

I'm no longer thinking about the strangeness when I'm walking Sherri to her door. I'm thinking about the required goodnight kiss, how I don't have time for more – whatever more might be – with my friend waiting, and I'm glad I don't when she grinds her lips and teeth into mine, pushing her hips into me. I'm not ready for this rapid switch from the casual to the carnal. I'm caught off guard, my back actually up against her door, behind which I imagine too well what might be happening even this deep in the night.

❧

Darlene and I make up half a singing foursome in a variety show. We're distinguished by red vests and an inability to harmonize. At the end of the show each of us is thinking we'll win first prize. Hadn't we stood up there on that huge stage in a town an hour and a half from home and sung "Michael"?

When third place goes to some kids, we're sure second will be ours. It goes to the guitar player, and a skit we didn't like wins first. Darlene sinks, perhaps because she knew we couldn't sing. Did she hope the other groups would be so bad that we'd be the last refuge of the judges? The other three of us feel we really weren't too bad. Or perhaps we were merely wishing we could get somewhere just by wanting it.

The fact is I can sing. Before I arrived in high school, my brother and I were always chosen to sing solos in the Christmas Concert version of "We Three Kings." I sing, "Myrrh is mine, its bitter perfume / breathes a life of gathering doom." I don't know what the words mean, but they're haunting, and I can make them vibrate in my shaky voice right through the one-room school. All the kids – Grades 1 to 8 – are standing in four rows on the stage around me. The green curtains on each side of the stage are pulled. No one behind them giggles and pokes and makes the material wiggle. Everyone is standing up here, singing carols between the skits. Our parents and friends are crunched into our desks. Some of the kids from other schools and from the high school have climbed up onto the half-wall that divides the one main room from the lobby, where everyone has hung winter coats and the boots are tumbled on the floor, wet from melted snow. A large stove in one corner – with a tin guard around it – sends out the heat. Peanuts, wool, books, breath – I'm surrounded by smells: chalk, hair, Christmas oranges, the green cleaning compound thrown on the wood floor to keep down the dust. All this I sing to from the third row left, not yet in the back row, reserved for the tallest, the ones who seldom open their mouths, except for my brother, whose voice is already a man's.

Our family sings in church, standing for the hymns. But we are not among those who carry the song up to the altar and beyond with the clear assuredness of some of the others, mainly women. My mother sings most sweetly when she sings along with radio carols, the Bay Christmas Choir, just before I leave for school in the morning. Her mother has died, and her father is sick as well. She is moved most of all by "Silent Night," and sings along in German. From her I learn how to cry at certain music. It feels as if I am coming into something distinctly my own, this melancholy at Christmas.

My father I hear humming when he bends to sharpen a saw clamped in the anvil. And he plays fiddle on winter nights, so he knows how to hear music and take it where the guitars can come chording along. But singing? The closest he gets is when he's with the other men, his part in the up and down buzz when he shares the story of a particular hunt. For there, hunting deer, seven or eight men keep attuned to one another yet stand a half-mile apart, a mile. Not all the men can hear this song easily, but those who can know exactly where the others are as they move through fields and bush, their white coats quiet against the snow.

Then comes the moment of rapture: the buck is sighted, fleeing with two does, and Lorne has a clear shot and doesn't miss. The rifle booms, and the hunters raise their voices one by one.

❧

Five of us gather at the front pew: Nert, Fly, Far-Off, me, and the pastor. I don't know why Nert bears her peculiar name. She's neither pretty nor ugly. Being the only girl, she has a lot to carry even though we generally tend to ignore her. Fly is patient, and while the pastor is extolling some point or other, he leans forward, arms on his knees, and waits for the flies to crawl into his hand. He's quick; I've seen him catch a fly and hold it through the pastor's talk. I believe he's deciding whether to kill the thing or not. I've seen him squeeze his fist until there's nothing. Other times he holds it till we're through and allowed out the church door, where he lifts his hand up and lets it go. I wonder how he makes such decisions, and whether it has something to do with what the pastor is telling us – about salvation and faith.

Far-Off is hardly ever here, having to come a long way, and even when he's in church, he seems to be elsewhere, with no real fear in him either for the pastor or for the things the pastor is telling us to fear. I, on the other hand, feel the power in the pastor's ideas, especially the notion of damnation. I cannot tell really if I'm afraid of the idea, of the pastor, of my family (what would they think if I were suddenly to disagree and decide my own course?), or of the church community who will assemble soon enough to see us confirmed in the faith. First they will expect to hear how well we have learned the essential creeds, special words, specific hymns, answers to long lists of questions. Then we will be given our first communion and our personal hymn books.

Because the church is a long way from my home, I've been sent to live with one of the congregation members. For two weeks I will open my mind and let the pastor fill it as he sees fit. I can't believe how long the days become as I sit in the church, on the hard pew, not merely for an hour, the length of the Sunday service, but four hours, without a break, listening and reciting. Nor can I believe the pastor when he marks an X beside the names of the Old Testament books I've spelled incorrectly. It should be enough that I remember them in the right order, never mind spelling Ecclesiastes. He's asking more than he has any right to, demanding what is technically not necessary for "true faith," and I feel offended and overburdened.

Pastor Bauer is a mild man, but there is a firmness in his handling of us that weakens me. He's capable of talking about creeds and prayers for hours. By developing a certain low rumbling in his voice he drums the knowledge directly into our spirits. I've yet to see him take off his suit jacket even though the air in the little church is stifling, barely alleviated by the half-open window near the altar through which the flies find their way.

At night when I lie in a strange bed, I imagine I'm not going to make it down the right path, will end in hell. In my little New Testament Gideon, on the page entitled "What Jesus Taught About Some of Life's Problems," I have these areas checked for special attention: Death, Forgiveness, Labour, Obedience, and Swearing. It seems I will survive only if I become a pastor, fingering my own special Bible with bright gold-trimmed pages and black leather binding at once sturdy and limp. It will fold back across my hands as I hold it open, a tasselled bookmark of green leather hanging down. I see myself in a black robe at the front of the church, turning to the altar to pray before ascending to the pulpit to say just what I think about God and those gathered below.

My mother says, "He preaches a good sermon," which I understand to mean he has something to say about her life here. Mostly I get carried away by the smells of the church, closed up for as long as three weeks and then opened to a congregation in formal wools; by the four white candles lit at the beginning of the service; by the organ up front taking us away into sorrow and joy; by the weave on my brother's dark brown dress pants; by the regulars I see nearly every third Sunday except sometimes in summer when the farms demand almost constant attention; by those who show up now and then, usually for Christmas, sometimes for Easter, the sons and daughters who've moved to the city or drifted away from the faith. I can watch from my seat between my mother and brother, if I'm not too obvious or fidgety in my rubbernecking.

My father makes no judgment about the pastor; he seldom speaks ill of anyone and so seems to be judging us all. My brothers wouldn't talk to me about such things, and I know better than to ask. But the pastor is under scrutiny. He's not the first to minister to this church; he has a standard to meet. What will, for example, the Three Sisters think of him? My mother doesn't tell me, maybe because I'm staying at the home of one of the sisters, Nert's mother.

All three sisters are believers, with the happiness of a faith that can stand up to poverty and ill health. Nert's mother is the least happy; she has the most difficult life of the three. Her husband has to work off the farm occasionally in winter. Also, he once belonged to another religion and still will not join our church even though for his wife's sake he married there and allows their children to attend. Almost completely bald, his head, whenever I see it, shines red. His face seems inflamed although, like his wife, he's always kind enough not to pay me much attention.

When the day of our communion arrives, I stand at the front of the congregation with Nert, Fly, and Far-Off, ready to answer all the questions. We do pretty well, right down to the eating of the bread and the drinking of the wine, overwhelmed by the solemnity and meaningfulness emanating from the families in the pews and from the pastor himself. We sing "Beautiful Saviour," accompanied by the organ played as quietly as possible. When the ceremony is over, we take our places in the front pew for the rest of the service, liberated from our families. We sit beside the pastor's wife; she's pregnant, a condition that intrigues me, since I can't really put the pastor together with an erection.

As I'm about to sit down, I see Nert's father in the back pew. He has snuck in, it seems. In his eye flashes a kind of terror, that he might turn and see the black priest of the other religion bearing down on him to warn of the soul-dangers of his surroundings. I also see anger and fear. Compelled by his wife to be here on his daughter's important day, he knows the pastor will grip his hand at the end of the service and lean eagerly towards him, keen to gather in a tardy member of the flock.

I hope to see such an exchange at the end of the service, but instead people gather around me, some of the women to give little kisses, to shake my hand. When the time comes to get through the door, I see nothing of Nert's father. The pastor is standing in his usual spot, shaking the hands of all who step out into the summer sun. He grips my hand and looks me in the eye as if for one last time. I, of course, am the one to look away. He's just too bountiful right now, too pleased with his charges, certain that none of us will ever sin again and that today really is the beginning of something.

Perhaps it's this willed power that Nert's dad cannot abide and that sends him walking briskly down the road, not waiting for his family. They'll catch up to him later in their old car, going back to the farm the pastor never visits. Maybe Pastor Bauer is not willing to risk the consequences of suffering open hostility on its home ground. Maybe he's just glad the children have come to him.

My father and the other men are already down the steps on the gravelly lawn, reaching into their dark suits for cigarettes. Handbags dangle from the arms of the women chattering in their group. I'm trying to feel as if I'm one of these people now, a newly made adult, someone who understands how to be comfortable with adult complexities. I'm trying, but I must not be trying hard enough.

❖

My parents have taken the train and left me with my brother, five years older, in charge. I can't tell which I'm more unhappy about: that my parents didn't take me or that my brother now has control. I start testing the boundaries on the drive home from the station.

We're driving through flat land and then dipping into a gully, across a bridge and up the other side. My brother's at the wheel of my father's car, the family car, our only car – a '58 Chev Impala. I push him to accelerate. He likes the idea, too, and with all the windows down, the scenery screams past us in a way I know can't be good. I feel guilty thinking of my father now, but then I imagine him on the train talking, pointing, settling in for the night – and I'm okay, free to push my brother.

At home I become more childlike. I refuse to do my own chores and now our parents' jobs as well: feeding, milking, cleaning, weeding, gardening, checking up at night. I tease him about girlfriends, and I can tell he enjoys himself when I list off the ones who like his looks.

We're in the final, washing-up stage of evening chores, meticulous with the cream separator that stands in the corner of the porch. We know the stink of sour milk and don't like it; we've been well trained. The shiny steel innards get washed in a large pan of dishwater. My brother has asked me twice now to pick up the tea towel and dry. I dance away until I'm puffing out my chest and saying, "Make me." And as I turn back, he slaps me with the dishcloth. It whips across my mouth and around my cheeks, a repulsive wet grey stink. Besides my pain (and surprise) it's the anger in his eyes that hurts. I run out of the house and into the yard, smarting that he's bigger, stronger, taller.

Later that summer we're pals again and heading home after the drive-in in his first car; we're always driving to get away from the farm. We've dropped off his girlfriend, the show behind us, a slow, colourful story about Elvis's happy life in the army, another world we know is unreal but like anyway. In the movie *I'm* starring in, I have the leading role, my brother the sidekick for a change. But looking out at the dark fields moving past, I can't imagine a film being made here. What would happen? There's just us, some farms, cows stuck up against a fence in a pasture that's nibbled down to the stones, and a big sky that runs its electric northern lights and leaves us wishing we were elsewhere.

Longing and monotony put me to sleep. I awake when my head flies forward and smacks the windshield. The neutral noise of car tires on gravel has changed to the rocky bouncing on stones that bang and scrape along the bottom of the car. I cry out and look down into the ditch we're dropping into, cutting a slow-motion swath through the long grass. The lights and nose of the car point towards the mud near the bottom. As I look back I see the source of the loud crash that awoke me: we've sliced off a telephone pole, which has fallen over behind us, only its wires keeping it from toppling completely.

My brother is hysterical, out of the car, frantic about his girlfriend, what will she say, will she stick with him now that he's wrecked his car? I can't see the point of that line of thought right now, and I realize I'll have to be the one to make sense here. I check to make sure we're okay. My head is sore but not bleeding. The right front fender is caved way in where it hit the pole. My brother's wailing. It's his first accident, and he needs the car for his work. He can't imagine coping without wheels. It's late, very late, the moonlight just enough to set the scene: two guys, a car in the ditch, a pole wobbling behind them, the sound of smashing still ringing in their ears.

I tell him over and over it's going to be okay. Now that the danger is past, I'm thrilled but scared. My brother doesn't seem to be able to move away from the car. He can't get beyond the moment. I tell him we have to walk to the farmhouse up ahead and call Dad.

"I can't!" he says, groaning; Dad is the last person he wants to tell. But what else can we do? I pull his arm, and soon we're walking down the road, then up a dark farm lane, worrying about a guard dog; then we're pounding on the farmer's door. We know who lives here – the Husacks – but we don't know them well. A man shouts from the other side: "Who is it?" We try to explain, and the word "accident" opens the door. The man looks as if he's prepared not for our sad story but for some terrible late-night deed. When my brother blurts out the tale, he ushers us to the phone.

First my brother talks to our mother, because she's the one who answers this late. I can see her standing in the hall with the phone in hand, knowing a late-night call is bad news. The official version – the right tire blew and pulled us into the ditch – forms quickly in my brother's mind. That's what he tells my father, now that he's gathered his wits and can speak like an adult, standing in a stranger's kitchen with the naked bulb showing every pale flutter in his face.

Dad accepts the story and is calm when he comes to pick us up. The arrangements about the car will come later; tonight we're relieved to be going home to our beds. At least I'm relieved. I'm not sure what my brother is feeling now that we're in Dad's car, the two of them in the front and me in the back. We aren't speaking because everything has been said, everything, that is, except what I know: that my brother fell asleep at the wheel. The sky is brightening in the east by the time we pull up to the house. Our mother is awake, waiting. She gives my brother a hug but doesn't cry.

Her question for me she reserves; she will ask what really happened later, sneaking the query in during unrelated conversation when I might not be on my guard. I will have to decide what to say, whose side I will be on. I might get blamed if the truth were to come out – perhaps my mother will tell me I should have stayed awake and not let my brother nod off, the wheel turning loose in his hands. She may not mean to blame me, but worry about the older son, who's moved out in the world, far from her protective love, will overpower her. He's the one to stew about, not me. Not yet.

❖

I can't get the hang of skating; possibly it's fear of water, of ponds with cattails sticking up through cracking ice.

So hockey's out. And baseball's just endless hours of standing, and then the ball's heading your way, all eyes waiting. Basketball in the auditorium goes astray when no adult comes to teach us. We degenerate into a game called war, its point to win goals by heaving the ball at one of the two exit doors guarded by your best goalie. A wonderful thumper of a game – until the hinges on the doors start lifting. The teachers stop the ruckus and turn us out into the cold.

But football. In the fall we put together a team and get one of the teachers to organize rides to and games with two other towns, each over an hour away. We have enough guys who can throw the ball, catch it, even kick it, but not really enough to make an offensive line. What we're mainly missing is someone who can hike the ball, which it turns out I can do. I'm not beefy enough to be a lineman, but I'm flattered by the praise the quarterback tosses my way.

Our first away game: 25–0 at halftime, 50–0 at the end. We're humiliated but still a little pleased we managed to pull together a team and survive a whole game. Plus we now have some idea of what we need to do better. From the other team we've learned plays, angles, attitudes, the need for shouts and determination. We also know how much we miss a coach. Yet our spirit stays good.

We get better. We win a few games. Once I catch the ball – I've switched for one game to end – the touchdown pass that wins the game in the final moments of the final quarter. The ball curves down, I'm running hard, the defence clawing at my back, my arms out, and the perfect parabola wins the day. It's all artistic and leaping joy right then. Mostly, though, it's heavy physical stuff. From the moment I put on the shoulder pads I feel the concrete weight of someone smashing into me.

I'm grateful for my helmet, an old one that's a bit too tight. I got it from a successful Blue Bomber who grew up in my area and whose family knows my parents well. It's alluring, that helmet. I don't wear it all the time – it makes the rounds among those who want to get the ball and grind up through the bodies for a yard or two. I don't wear it if I'm playing end, but down at centre I sure do. Sometimes we call ourselves the Ghosts – for our ability to vanish from the scoreboard? When we're losing and getting smashed around, I wish we were the Gossamers and could just slip by everyone.

It's raining, and the mud of the field helps the other team, it seems, with their fancy cleats and better equipment. You stare across the line at someone. Sometimes you know he's already a man, with a man's anger, the thrill in his eyes there because he can run into you hard. I do my best, but he runs over me, pressures the quarterback into early misfires.

The rain comes down in my eyes as I'm lying there. The guard next to me is hurt: two linemen from the other side have ganged up on him, why we don't know. It doesn't seem to have anything to do with the strategy of the game. A pecking order has been established, and they're going after our guard, a nice guy, quiet, big enough but not when two goons are coming at him. It's all meanness now.

Our fullback, Ron, knows what to do. He's not big but strong, the kind of hard, short strength you can count on to get a yard when you really need it. He convinces the huddle to listen to him. We're going to run an end play, but Ron isn't going to carry the ball, the QB will. Ron's going to go up the middle and slam into the bully we agree deserves it most, the flabby one with a big mouth and a hanging lip.

I hike, and the action rolls right. Just before the play slows up, Ron drives and sinks his shoulder into the gut of the other guy. Who whooshes wildly and sinks down, doubled up, the wind knocked out of him. For a moment I think he might piss himself, he looks so helpless, so deserving of punishment. We're immediately vindicated and pleased. Their coach comes out from the sidelines but says nothing to us. We expect the blocks to get more personal, and I worry about Ron, but nothing more happens. Point taken, I suppose.

We lose the game but win the moment. We remember that moment on the bus ride home, our smelly gear around us. We know how good and powerful it feels to look after our own. But now it will take our teachers, our friends, our parents, our dogs, long unbroken stretches of our silent selves to make us gentle again.

❖

This Halloween we have only three options: to dress up as old women and get candy from the town merchants, or not, or to put that kids' stuff behind us altogether and burn tires in the middle of the street. Once the night gets into our blood, it's easy to be bad. Our town's so small there're no cops, the only detachment an hour away on mostly gravel roads, so if we care to – and some of us do – we can make this Halloween one worth remembering.

None of this would be happening, none of this organizing by daylight and running at night, if it weren't for Schneck. He's a big kid who arrived here in August from somewhere on the British Columbia coast, where he got into gang trouble. His parents sent him here to live with his aunt. She's not an easy person to manipulate, as Schneck must know by now; he doesn't bother her at all. Instead, he finds us with time on our hands, just waiting for someone to lead us into temptation.

We aren't a gang but something close, six of us, and our target is a teacher we don't like. Schneck has us gathering the necessary materials: eggs, beet juice, crankcase oil. First, to fire up our zeal, we break into the high school, prying open a window and hefting one another up to the ledge. While little kids hop house to house trick-or-treating, we're tipping up chairs, throwing papers from the teacher's desk into the garbage pail and lighting them on fire. Next we're cutting up the flag. Each of us gets a chance to rip up red. Schneck has a big knife, and he's first at slashing.

There's something good in this heart-racing connection with other guys, the relief of getting done the wickedness we talked about, the ease of swearing and shouting out loud in the dark classroom. Then we're cutting across the playing field, getting ready to hit the teacherage, the nice white house where the dislikeable teacher lives with his wife and one skinny kid. He makes fun of Schneck in front of other students. Schneck should be in Grade 10 with the rest of us, but he's failed a grade, and now he's one of those big handfuls whose wide shoulders draw down the scorn of the teachers.

Now the teacher will be the one scorned. One of us knocks on his door. When he opens it, we pelt him with eggs. At least two hit the mark and drive him back inside. Then we come out of the dark trees and run along the house, throwing the beet juice and oil as high as we can across the white siding. We shout incoherently, noises intended to strike fear in the teacher. I know immediately that we have crossed a line and that Mother didn't have this in mind when she left me to have fun on my own.

When we gather at the end of the lane under the half-light of the only street light in that part of town, Schneck is jubilant. None of us wavered when it came to the attack. The rest of us are ready to go home, already starting to worry, trying to imagine what will happen next. We make up a story about some other kids who attacked the teacherage; but there are no other kids: we're the obvious crew, and everybody could tell we were trouble. We throw away the containers, the matches, and Schneck folds up his knife.

We make a pact not to talk, but the appearance of the cop car in town the next day sends all of us, except Schneck, into panic. Schneck makes us swear to stick together, but the first guy into the car – the very first to sit there and feel the weight of the cop looking down on him – tells everything, which makes it easy for the rest of us. We hardly have to speak, just nod and sign, and some of us are relieved. Now we're expected to show contrition because it's not enough just to admit guilt, and contrition means scrubbing off the teacherage with a brush, in the freezing November cold, our fingers growing stiff. It means facing my father, who says nothing but looks at me as if I'm worse than stupid. It means taking time off school and going down the road to the big town to face a judge.

In court my parents stand behind me in their best clothes, as if at a funeral, while the judge listens to the officer's report. The judge must know we're scared; apparently everyone can tell. The entire town's saying we're going to get our asses kicked for being unthinking punks not smart enough to see where vandalism leads. Some are surprised we were so easily duped by Schneck, whom they see rightly as the ringleader. The school janitor, as he sits in the café, tells his version over and over: how he opened the classroom in the morning and found the room a mess, the flag ripped and burned. We didn't burn the flag, didn't go that far, but we know it's best to keep quiet now. The judge hears our story and grows livid – our lack of respect for the flag shows an absence of moral character. He believes he might stop us from turning into something worse than juvenile delinquents. This is his chance to drag us back into the fold.

His anger spills onto my parents, and the parents of the other boys also standing here. We are all looking down, not bold any more, trying not to blush, even Schneck. And we get off with a warning, even Schneck, because no one tells on him. No one says it was his idea, his doing, his fault. We hang together at least that much even when some parents demand that we betray him – but they don't have to live with him at school. We all feel almost happy to be free.

One kid in our group, who is sixteen, gets a stiffer judgment because he's supposedly an adult. He stands up alone after the five under-age offenders have been reprimanded, and he takes a tongue-lashing about proper civic responsibility from the judge, who gives him a suspended sentence.

My parents and I have little to talk about on the drive home. I almost hope the rumour about Schneck getting sent back to B.C. is true. He's too charismatic for us; we're too ready to follow him. I watch the winter countryside grow dark. My parents don't bother to stop in town today for any reason. Whatever we might need – mail, coffee, gas, flour – can wait until the storm of gossip dies down.

When we meet again, the six of us, we'll have to join together for a while to save ourselves from the ridicule and laughter of the other kids at school. We'll have to listen to the janitor yelling at us if we so much as drop an orange peel. We'll have to learn how to hold ourselves back from Schneck until we find out more about who we are and who we're going to be – the decent good guys, surely, that everyone, ourselves included, seems to be hoping for.

◆

My essay "Should Canada Acquire Nuclear Weapons?" wins unanimous applause from our three teachers. Four years ago, when Sputnik flew over, everything changed, I know that. Around that time I found pieces of silvery tinsel in the pasture, and I knew the Russians had put them there on purpose, for espionage. Everything else was as it should have been – poplars, cow paths, darting waxwings – but those man-made strips that surely fell out of the sky made me feel insecure.

That's what I remembered when I wrote, "In the case of a nuclear war, nuclear weapons would, of course, be purchased directly from the United States. However, in the event of a war would Canada have time enough to transport these nuclear arms into Canada in order to make a defensive stand? It does not seem likely." I was proud of the way I was able to be clear without getting too involved in thinking.

Ready for a new writing challenge, I discover rhyming couplets. I love to anticipate the end word, and I like the way the rhyme gives me a hint of what I'm going to say. "In Her Heart" is the story of two young people just out of high school who marry, but fight because they're poor: "Then she flew into a wicked rage and called him a no-good cheat / He slapped her hard and kissed her soft, and left in the noonday heat." I keep the poem going as long as I can, galloping towards true unhappiness. It's thirty-four lines long when I'm done. The girls I work with on the yearbook like it.

"It should definitely go in," the assistant editor says. From that moment I look at her in a new way.

But we have to show everything to the principal first. I sign the poem "Our Shakespeare" before I hand it to him. When he reads it, he's convinced I've stolen it. The girls rush to my defence.

Later my mum and dad read the poem and seem pleased. But I think they like the nuclear warfare essay better, and they are only interested, it seems, in *what* I'm saying. Neither appears impressed with the way I've kept the poem going right to the end. "He hated his job so he cursed his life and the very day he was born." And then the tragedy: "The day before she had learned a fact, and had meant to tell him sweetly" – tell him, of course, that she's pregnant. My parents have seen other poems of mine, from grade school, so maybe they're expecting something more along the lines of the one I published in *The Western Producer*, but "Heartbreak Hunt" doesn't deal with the tough social issues of the real world I'm living in.

My dad reads *The Western Producer* not just for the prices of grain and pork but also for the stories about farmers, ranchers, workers, animals. The section full of stories is the one he likes best, the same section that devotes part of a page to young people and what they have to say. One corner features poems by children, who use pen names. For some reason no poem is published under the author's real name.

I try not to remember too clearly why I picked my pen name: Mr. Whippoorwill. It's too soft, an embarrassment, I know that now. What would the girls think if they knew? But Mr. Whippoorwill's poem was printed, and my father read it. My poem was in the paper.

I still stop and listen when I hear the bird's call as I walk home in the dark, but I'd never use his name for my own, not now. I wouldn't use a pen name at all; or if I had to, it would be something harder, like Mr. Sputnik. I know why the whippoorwill isn't in my collection of Red Rose birds, and I'm not surprised by this omission. He's all song, sweet but unseen, as insubstantial as a voice in a dream, some fairy-tale child's bird.

❖

The test for my driver's licence was easy: all I had to do was drive to the post office and back. Everyone assumed I knew how to drive. I was, after all, a farm kid, up on the Massey-Ferguson first with my dad, then with my brothers, then on my own. At fourteen, I drove the wheat-laden truck in from the threshing machine to the granary, rear wheels sinking down through the stubble. I shovelled the grain off the truck – and got it done quickly enough to be back out to the field in time for the next load.

I'd take a handful of wheat and chew it till it got gummy, pull-start the auger, back the truck into position, and slowly ease up the trap door so the grain wouldn't flood the hopper. I'd make sure its head was pushed deep in the granary to keep the grain from piling up near the

door. Sometimes I had to be sweating in two places at
once: in the back of the truck and in the granary, the chaff
from the wheat filling my nose, itching under my shirt.

But when that work was done, I'd get to drive the
weightless, bouncing truck across the field. I'd run up to
the mound of yellow straw that kept getting bigger with
each load of stooks the farmers hauled in, their horses
sometimes spooking alongside the roaring machine and
the taut belt that ran out to the tractor pulley.

My dad isn't one of the stook haulers, and he doesn't
handle the grain except to run his hands under the wheat
now and then to test its hardness as it pours into the back
of the truck. He's the boss of the machine, making sure
the belts are the right tension, keeping the nipples
greased. Sometimes he climbs up on top to turn a wheel
and raise the snout out of which the straw is blowing.
When he comes down to talk to me, telling me to bring
some tea from the house, he yells out of the side of his
mouth, making himself heard above the roar of the
shakers that separate the straw from the grain and the
howl of the fans that blow the straw out.

All day he works in this noise, never escaping to the far
corner of the field where the stook haulers can be quiet
for a while, walking alongside their horses, building the
loads on their racks. Because he's the man entrusted with
making sure the machine – the huge machine that roars
and thrums and shakes – works through the day, he stops
only when the fields are empty, near dark, when the men
turn their horses and racks back to the house and the big
meal my mother's prepared.

My father never misses the threshing. But this year, before the final harvest begins, he's sick, so grey he goes to the hospital in the little town north of us. He hadn't planned on staying, just wanted something from the doctor to help. But the doctor tells him he needs to stay a few days. After he's been assigned a bed, we say goodbye.

I drive home, feeling grown up. My mum's looking out her window. It's ten miles east on a gravel road, then ten miles south, a lot of it washboard, the dust billowing behind us.

The next day we're back at the hospital. He's sitting up in bed. He still looks grey. I can't help thinking he looks ridiculous here, without his farm clothes. The ward is small, only three other beds, two empty. The other patient, even worse-looking than my father, gazes out the window, not bothering to turn and see who we are. The entire time we are there, he doesn't sit up. No nurses or doctors come by.

My parents talk quietly, as if they don't want to disturb him. I sit and listen but my mind soon wanders. They're going over details about what the doctor told him, about bills and chores, about who's sent get-well wishes. It's as if they're still in the kitchen at home.

When we're almost ready to leave, Dad turns to me. "You'll have to cut the oats," he says. "It's ready." Then he tells me what I'll need to do. I know he's only talking about the forty acres south of the house, but this is still a big job. Bigger than I want, actually. The binder is a complicated machine, temperamental in the way it cuts the grain. When I've driven the tractor that pulls the binder,

Dad has sat on the binder itself, adjusting the levers and making sure the twine comes off its spool correctly, binding the sheaves before dropping them for us to pick up later and prop together into stooks. You can work the levers from the tractor, too, but it works best with two.

On the way home, I realize I haven't really understood why Dad is in hospital. I assume it's his ulcer. It's impossible to imagine anything else. I think of the nights he's been up, stirring some milk concoction in the kitchen. He can't eat Mum's fresh-baked bread and waits instead for the dried, day-old — sometimes even older — slices, which he soaks in milk. Something's happening now that they both know about but don't tell me.

We're hardly back in the yard when Mum takes up her chores, kerchief knotted tight under her chin. She misses him, but she's also angry that he's sick. And she's worried, and she blames him for what our family calls his low pain threshold. She tells me finally, a basket of eggs on her arm, that he's not going to have a serious operation, that he should be home within the week.

When I study the binder, I try to remember what he told me: to make sure the table is level, the blade greased, the ball of twine loose but tight. He assumed I'd been paying attention. He said that if the weather was hot and dry, I should begin, shouldn't wait for my brothers to come home on the weekend, couldn't count on the weather to wait for them.

My brother-in-law takes his holidays and comes out from the city, but he knows even less than me. It's not easy without Dad. If only he were here, where we could ask him questions. We have trouble adjusting the canvas table the grain drops onto, after the grain's been cut by the blade behind the guard. The lever is stuck. I imagine other problems if we solve this one. That's when my friend drives in. His dad, hearing that my dad is in hospital, sent David over to help.

"We don't use a binder any more ourselves," he says, "but anyway here's what you're doing wrong." We had the canvas on incorrectly. He shows us how to adjust the table, points to where the grain will bung up if it's too green or a little wet. Before he leaves, he says, "You should tell your dad it's time to move on to a swather."

We're finally up and running, learning as we go. I handle the steering wheel of the tractor with my left hand and lean back and work the levers of the binder with my right. I stop now and then to check the twine ball. I'm careful to make the corners neat, since it's easy for the grain to slide under the blade when I'm turning. I stop often to adjust the table so that it's higher than the stones but still as low as possible, especially in the patches where water pooled after seeding and the grain didn't grow high or yield well.

I'm impatient to be done, not because I have other chores but because I fear some part of the machine will buck and break and leave us again to our own resources, which are slim without my father's expertise at hand. I've started at the outer edges of the field, closing in on the centre, making smaller and smaller trips until I'm left with only a thin, rectangular patch in the middle. The sheaves are dropping successfully, the twine holding the grain secure. I relax, thinking about what David said.

Soon nobody will be working this way any more: we'll leave the binder and threshing machine behind. Other farmers are pouring money into combines that mean one man with one machine can harvest his fields on his own – no more stooks, no more threshing gangs.

My dad should be here. If this is the last time we use the binder, he would definitely want to be here. But the tractor is waiting for me to go forward, to finish, so carefully, gradually, I let out the clutch.

❖

Grade 12 math takes a leap I haven't anticipated. The teacher talks about logarithms, and I feel the outside world lurch closer. We've been a protected handful who come to this brick school every day and learn to sit together, when really we want to get outside to talk or smoke or replay that lovely moment when the football makes its graceful trajectory from the quarterback. Trajectory I can see is a concept of some use, but logarithms seem a mind game only the teacher is enjoying, and sometimes he looks worn out with explaining and examples.

I'd like to be as unruffled as the teacher. He wears a tie. I've seen him without it only once or twice, when he's eating at the café in town. He lives at the back of the café, where out-of-town male teachers always stay, getting room and board. Which means not a lot of privacy, having to eat where everyone else eats. So either he's at school teaching or doing his paperwork, or he's in his room letting his thoughts fly free, far from the students and their parents. Sometimes he packs up his VW Beetle and drives off, back to his old life, I suppose, though we can't imagine he had one before he came here to stand before us, speaking the gibberish of sines and cosines.

Grey flannel pants, dark blue sports coat which he removes, white shirt and tie, wavy dark hair he runs his fingers through when the dumb ones in our class can't get it. I thought I was one of the smarter kids because I can exchange ideas with the teachers when they want some fun, usually on Fridays. I imagine becoming someone like the teacher one day, as smart as he is. I want the clothes: crisp, new, not bought through Eaton's mail-order catalogue with the hope of a decent fit.

I want to be someone I can be sure about. So I dig into math. I don't do well. I begin to think he isn't telling me some elementary rule, the key that others seem to be grasping. I don't like feeling stupid. In English 11 the final question on the provincial exam asked, "Was Macbeth a bloody butcher? Discuss." I said yes, of course, he killed all those people. My grade was 50R, meaning someone reread the paper in light of my good grades otherwise and decided to pass me, hoping this brush with failure would jolt me out of the literal into an appreciation of ambiguity and ambivalence.

At home I fling my books around, yelling what can't be said in class: "I can't do this damn stuff!" My mother tells me throwing won't help, but she's worried, too. She can't help, that's the unspoken truth, since she never went beyond Grade 2, a fact that fuels my education. She won't tolerate anything less than my completing high school — after that it's a void for her. University is too much to imagine, so maybe a job, or teacher training. But first this hurdle.

Sometimes the tears come, tears of rage. I don't want to learn these equations. Can't I be the student who goes to the next level without this knowledge? Can't there be an exception based on my individuality? I will never take a math course in university, so why should I need it here?

Even more worrisome: the teacher grows distant. I worry he's giving up on me. His teaching is fair, he never plays favourites, yet I think in his secret marking heart he must have room to manoeuvre. When a test comes back, he leaves no margin for encouragement in the black and white world of math. What is right is checked, what is wrong gets an X. The good marks are totalled, placed above 100, written on the front page. Mine is not the worst grade this time, but I feel as if he's not paying attention to me. I want to pour the burden of my frustration into his cuticle-clean, chalk-dusty hands. I want him to take my problem away.

Then a classmate — one of the few bound for elsewhere, beyond this small town and these lonesome farms — relates a story that shocks me. The teacher has been seen with a young woman from another town. Seen — by whom I never think to ask — with her in the back seat of his VW. My friend spends some time sketching the picture, the cramped difficulties and the larger problem of not being able to invite the girl back to the café.

When the teacher walks into class the next day, I look

at him differently. I see I'm going to have to figure out some problems on my own. I wonder if this is how it's going to be from now on. He hasn't changed – same expansive manner, same energy aimed at getting us through the curriculum, same clothes, same authority – but now there's something else. Where is that new part, screwing in the back of a VW, when he's talking about transposing and logic? Inside him he's nurturing a memory not visible today. He's not going to mention or even allude to certain events. He's the same, and I wonder: to remain in one place when a part of you is already elsewhere, longing for something you must keep hidden – is that ambiguity? Or ambivalence?

Mrs. Martin in the municipal office is one of the nicest women I know. She's kind, listens carefully, answers clearly. She handles documents that bind men like my father and their farms to some other force besides the land and the weather. Dad pays taxes but never blames Mrs. Martin for taking his money. He respects her, says she's smart and easy to deal with, organized, above all honest. I know my father will be more likely to support my plan to attend university if she provides a reference in support of my bursary application.

Also, of course, it matters that she's a somebody. My mother or Mrs. Zalesnak, the neighbour down the road, could write a reference, but who are they? Mrs. Martin stamps paper, witnesses agreements, keeps track of changes to land deeds. I've already asked for the support of my English teacher, and I know she'll write a passionate letter. When she reads aloud to us, something flows out of her and into me. She declaims Shakespeare from a thin blue ill-used book handed down from student to student, often chucked in a desk with sandwiches and bits of orange and apple cores. The smell combines the mustiness with ink and paper, a mixture just right for listening as she walks back and forth in front of the class, book held high, the hem of her skirt unravelling. I recognize urgency in her voice, the demand that we love this language as she loves it, the assurance that if we do, it will save us somehow. The yearning she strikes up in us – in me, anyway – is balanced by the smell of the book itself, to remind me that grottiness has its place, too.

I won't be taking English when (if) I get to university. I'll have to chart a course more directly aimed at future employment, something that my father can understand. I'll pick chemistry, zoology, biology, requirements for becoming an ornithologist. My father can see the ultimate value in this goal although I know he's skeptical; he can't imagine someone spending his time working with birds. Who would pay such a person? I have to remember who he is, a man who more frequently says things that make me realize he, like so many of his age, is fed up – with the world, the government, the weather, with crops that don't yield well.

Mrs. Martin's office is set back from the wide dusty street in town. When I open the door, she's at her desk behind the counter. I smell the oiled floor warmed by sunshine coming through the windows. She stands and approaches me, smiling.

"I want to go to university in September, and I need a reference for a bursary. Would you write one for me?"

"Yes, of course," she says. "Not many students from here go on in school, do they?"

I hand her the paper and she glances at it.

"I'll mail this in tomorrow," she says, returning to her desk, always with much to do. She studies me for just a moment. "You'll be leaving Mrs. Martin behind now."

This is news to me – a revelation. She means it as a joke, I think, but something tinges her words, something just short of bitterness. She herself has never gone to university, so perhaps it's some unfulfilled desire. It's never occurred to me that she might want something other than the life she has here, so central to things and so admired.

"Thank you," I say, trying not to show surprise. Because of course she's right. I will be leaving her behind. I simply hadn't thought of it that way. I hadn't thought of leaving anything behind.

One night, in bed, it hits me that I'm here, in this bed, for the last time. I listen as the house settles down. I'll catch a ride to the city with my brother in the morning; I'll be staying with him at first. He works as a mechanic in the B/A station across from the big CNR terminal. It's busy, a hub. A huge hotel stands in the background. Rich people arrive on the train and my sister's boyfriend, a redcap, hustles their bags. My sister works down the street in one of the skyscrapers, typing and filing insurance policies.

Already I'm nostalgic. It catches me unawares. For a moment I see both ways, ahead into what might happen and back through what has been. I think of the whippoorwill that follows me down the lane from the road late at night. When my friend drops me off, once his car's out of sight, no light appears except the wide blare of the Milky Way. The soft depths of its cool swirling dark make me walk a little off balance for a while.

I know you can't see the stars in the city. And who will hear the whippoorwill, if not me? I wonder about my mum. The last of her kids leaving home. I can feel she doesn't want to let me go. These last few days I've been happy to work with her, seeking out chores I once hated, like picking raspberries from the seven rows of canes. I've imagined there's something she's about to tell me, some word, some plan, some hope.

It's different with my father. He seems to be speeding towards a goal far ahead of him that grows increasingly private. When he says goodbye, we don't hug. It's my mother who gives me the comfort of her body. My father lifts his cap, wipes his face with his big red hand, and says, "Work hard."

They wave at the car as we drive off. Of course I'll be back; it's not as if I'm leaving forever. Not for Labour Day, though. Not for quite a while. Maybe not even until Thanksgiving.

# — THE CITY —

The first person I meet at university, Paul, doesn't seem to know anyone either. When he has his father's Impala, we drive out to the spillway built to save the city from its flooding river. We gaze at the water, then drive home. We have no beer to help. Neither of us understands the stooped professor who says he hopes we will open the door and walk into Kant's house one day. Each philosopher makes sense until he's refuted by a wiser man. Paul asks, How do you get to know girls in a philosophy class? It's all too much to think about.

By second term I meet a woman who seems to be my girlfriend but isn't, not yet — just a friend who likes to talk. We go to movies, and she teases me, and introduces me to her friends. I like them because they're seriously grappling with their courses. They walk with the professor from class to his office, seeking clarification. They wear sweaters with letters, and pointed dark glasses much like my own. Often they eat in the cafeteria, where I don't often go since I have my own bag lunch. I can't ease into the idea that after high school everyone goes on to university and does well.

The university provides scholarships to bright students from elsewhere – Bart, for example, from Zambia. He wears a sports coat and tie, like a teacher, beneath a big winter coat, the puffy layer he needs to keep warm under our frozen skies. He loves to probe, so the professors spar with him and his girlfriend, Dorothy, in political science. I hear of these debates from my girlfriend, who's in class with them while I'm mulling my way through philosophy and history. I haven't caught their sense of mission. I worry that I might not change, and that I might.

I sometimes hear Bart speaking from a stage to a group of students below. His long arms, the confidence so easily conveyed, the fun – he's brilliantly himself and other than us. But I can't tell if we listen because he's himself or because he's African. It could be both: I have no one to compare. The students believe him. Something about him makes them turn and listen. Is it his accent, his ties, his manner? Is he putting us on?

I'm spellbound by his skin, stretched tight over the bones of his face. I've never met a black man before, and Bart's face shines; his hair, eyes, palms, the shape of his head make me aware of my own body in a new way. As if I'm suddenly pudgier, less durable.

Bart is two years ahead of me, and when I'm learning

medieval history, he's facing a different problem entirely. He and Dorothy, my girlfriend tells me, are breaking up.

"But why?" I ask. They seem happy together, they're about to graduate with honours, they appear to believe the same things.

"Bart's going back to Zambia," she says.

I ask why he doesn't stay here, which must be, I think, better than there. Some arrogance must slip onto my face, for she says, "It's his home." Still, I can't help thinking: he has to go back, after all he's experienced here? Does he want to go home?

Having found this capital city in the provinces, how can I think otherwise? Before I met Bart I knew Zambia only as a country that drew my attention because it belongs to the rare Z group: zebra, Zorro, zero, Zieroth.

I wonder if I could live any place other than here – this city, the farm, the countryside flung out everywhere: birds, sky, wind, trees, patchwork crops. I have some fanciful knowledge – speculation my specialty – of London and Berlin. But Lusaka, the capital of Zambia? Wouldn't it be easier for Bart to continue his life of attention and thought rather than returning to what awaits him, presumably something harder?

The next time I see Bart with one of the professors, I try to grasp the distance he's come. But I fail: he's too comfortable here, with his courses, his professors, his Dorothy. My own small stretch – from farm to city, from the word that my uncle calls Negroes to my admiration for the rare flower of Bart – is only now becoming manageable. Which is why I will think of the happiness of his homecoming rather than the melancholy of his leaving us behind.

◆

The summer after my first year of university, I long to be changed. I've wandered through the academic year half in love with the new world and half sick at leaving the old. At Christmas break I almost packed in the book life, but I had nothing else to do and the surprising, occasional pleasure of learning held me to the books.

What this first summer really means is work: finding it, living it, making enough to get through the next year somehow. I apply for jobs as soon as classes are through, before the last of the final exams. I walk up to big glass buildings on streets like Broadway, apply for jobs such as grounds maintenance worker, filling in spaces to explain why I want this job and what qualifications I offer. I smile at receptionists, they smile at me. Sometimes I talk to employment officers. We smile our smiles although theirs mean something entirely different from mine. Half the jobs I apply for I don't want; the other half I won't get. After a few weeks of futility I think fondly of university again, of the small freedom of skipping classes.

Then I land a job at Versatile Manufacturing. I'm relieved and ambivalent. I have the coveted thing – summer job – but I'm not sure I can do the work, and the wages aren't great: no union. I qualify because I'm willing to work for poor pay. The first morning I get off the Pembina Avenue bus at six and find myself walking with several other men. Some are young like me, although not students, and some are older, gripping black lunch kits and wet-looking, hand-rolled cigarettes. No one says anything. The June morning is bright. I suspect they know too well what awaits them. It awaits me, too, but I recognize a summer job as only a stop on the way to real life. I can see in the men's faces that even the temporary can last longer than desired.

Versatile manufactures tractors, combines, and other farm equipment in a vast corrugated tin building that stretches high and far. We make our way to the main office, are given time cards and told who to talk to on the floor. I line up and get my card punched by the clock machine, a noise so sharp and loud I feel my hand is in danger. By the time I reach the floor, the racket has increased deafeningly. Great hooks and chains hang from girders up near the rafters. Men are operating machines that stamp sheets of metal into the shapes of other machines; men are sending sparks flying; men are hammering and firing metal. All men: there are one or two women in the office, but they don't come down to the floor.

Only one man carries papers. He can't be everywhere at once, and I learn to watch for his sudden appearance at my side. On that first endless morning, he seems to keep an eye on me. I've been teamed with Joe. Our job is to put the final nuts and bolts on tractor frames before they go to the paint shop. Large hulking carcasses of metal and metallic innards come slowly down the assembly line towards us. We attach bolts at key places smartly enough not to impede the forward motion. I work on one side and Joe on the other. I reach in and turn the wrench, tightening; then Joe comes to check. Sometimes the bolts aren't tight enough, and he tells me so. Sometimes I over-torque, and my hand pulls the wrench off the bolt. I bleed but not so that I need first aid. I notice Joe is wearing gloves as well as a smirk when I yelp and inspect my oozing knuckles. He enjoys my ineptitude and comments on my soft hands.

It takes time before he accepts that I can do this job, can handle the long stretch in the afternoon when the clock doesn't move, that I can drag up the energy needed to keep my end of the assembly moving. He knows when and how to work fast, how much to complete before coffee, when to knock off but still look busy. These are new skills.

Once he talks about the farm he had. "I sold it because I didn't want to work outside all the time," he says. I'm alert for regret or irony, but he has a face and a tone that keep his secrets safe.

Joe never asks about me. I've noticed this tendency in older men – my father among them – simply to turn away. And I have few opportunities to mingle with the others in the plant except at the half-hour lunch break and at wash-up before going home.

One day at lunch I follow the young men pouring through a side door. It's not a real door – we have to stoop – merely part of the corrugated tin wall cut out and hinged, its purpose unknown. Outside, two young men are loudly insulting each other, circling with knuckles raised. One steps in and smashes the other's head. The sound is sharp, liquid, sickening, calling up a low moan of appreciation from the crowd. The other hits back in a flurry of thrown fists, jerked heads, feet scuffling dirt. Other men shout encouragement or outrage until one fighter leaps upon the other and they roll on the ground among the boots of the watchers.

I gather from the threats and curses that these two have a long-standing quarrel — about what is unclear. The violence is so close I fear that I might be drawn in, that one of the other men might turn to me and say something that would require too much of me. I stay near the door, ready to retreat to the relative safety of Joe's taciturn nature. Later, when I tell him about the fight, he looks at me but says nothing, aligned with the fist fighters in some way I don't understand.

At wash-up we gather to get the oily gunk off before punching out. A large metal basin that can accommodate nearly all the men at its periphery shoots warm water out from a circle of fountains. Below are the spigots we pump to get industrial-strength pink soap on our hands, many of them blackened and cut, twisted and caked, nasty-looking appendages that don't seem a part of us and yet are as individualized, as fundamental, as our faces.

The spigots occasion a good deal of sexual comment; the end of the day, with its foretaste of freedom, produces horseplay and shoving, strutting and one-upmanship. I'm reminded of the cows at the trough as they bunt one another, jockeying for position, eager to get their noses into the cool well water. Except here the air is tinged with metal fumes and male sweat and harsh detergent and the real threat of rage.

I work through June, into July, struggling every evening into bed before anyone else because I have to get up and catch the first bus down Pembina. I can't make myself see the long view: that I get off each day earlier than most workers, that this is a summer job, not my life. Instead, I feel the injustice of giving my time and body for a salary that almost isn't worth it, a bare scratch above minimum. I've felt hard done by before, and irritated, but now I've moved beyond irritation to worry that a future of coarseness and tedium, exhaustion with little reward, is all that awaits me.

Then a friend gets me a job at Canada Packers. My wages double – the workers are unionized – and on my first morning I work on the cat food line with women. We're all dressed in white uniforms (our street clothes safely stowed in rows of clanking lockers). Soon the cat food cans – still warm from the sealing machine – come rolling down the line through a bit of glue, over a label that the glue picks up so that the label wraps itself around the can. We take the cans, wipe off excess glue, pack them in boxes.

The foreman, with flapping white coat, tie, and – I note – soft-looking hands, drifts by to half whisper in my ear: "Don't let the cans burn your hands." I'm confused: they're not that hot. I look to the women, and one takes pity and tells me in a kindly way that the foreman expects me to work faster.

I get moved around: from cat food to dog food to trimming off the mould that grows on the carcasses. I do not, mercifully, get nearer to the slaughtering of animals. I see their quivering entrails. I scoop hearts, kidneys, and livers into the machine that pulps them into wieners. A strong smell lingers about the place, an oily mixture of blood and fear and stockyard and propane and wet cardboard that settles in my clothes.

I recognize the men who do the killing; there're only a few of them, and they're easy to spot. They stride through the plant in high rubber boots. Management will not dare hassle them because they're kings, their long stiff yellow aprons wet and gleaming. Dangling from their belts are the electric stunners and long knives. Sometimes they come into the lunchroom to eat hamburgers. They sit by themselves; no one joins them. One has his locker near mine, and at the end of the day, when we change into street clothes, I watch him turn from killer back to citizen. His face doesn't change: it remains impassive, sealed.

In my fourth week, we go on strike. The plant shuts down. The issues are complex – wages, seniority, conditions – and won't be resolved before the end of summer. There's too little time left till classes to look for another job, so I take the train home.

When my father meets me at the station, I can't help but study him. I've seen him butcher a pig, a sacrament compared with the butchery at Canada Packers. His face doesn't seem to ache from the work he's done. He seems remote, sure, stolid, apparently satisfied.

The next day we're silent together in the open field, stacking hay bales under a blue sky. Now of course I'm working for nothing except meals and (I don't mind admitting) the pleasure of helping out, far from the difficulties awaiting me in the city. It feels as if I've been away from the farm – from home – much longer than one winter. I've changed – and here's my father, who seems not to have changed at all. Yet this steadfastness is no longer an irritation. It's like learning that white is made up of all the colours. Where I once took his calm for unbending conservatism, for locked-up views that had no further need of what the world might offer, I now see that this calm combines all sorts of qualities. And that some of them I might usefully try to acquire myself.

❖

At night mice scramble in the walls, and silverfish run for the bathtub drain when I switch on the light. I'm living on my own, if this is really on my own – with the mice, the vermin, and the Italians upstairs who, quiet all day, party all night, the men booming, the women shrieking, the babies crying, their language rolling easily through the walls and ceiling. It's enough to make me reflect on money, on not having it, my tiny bursary enough just to encourage me, my student loan growing by the week. When I first saw this big furnished room and combined kitchen with a bath to the side, it seemed the place for me: within walking distance of the university, and with a big bay window that made me feel I could do good work here. Now, daily, it seems more tawdry, small, even dirty. I resolve to spend my time in the library.

I'm working on second-year courses now. The classes are smaller, which makes me more aware that I scarcely know the right thing to wear or how to comb my hair. I'm afraid my inadequacies will show. Still, sometimes I lose track of them, caught up as I am by the colourful professors: the man who teaches Victorian poetry using Coles Notes, the rotund history prof who convinces his students that all life leaps from Europe, the blind Shakespearean scholar with the big Braille book who breaks off his lecture early when his dog needs to pee. I could never have imagined these men. I've entered a world of style and passion, and I move with the masses of students who sweep into corridors where lockers swell and bulletin boards announce bargain sales on textbooks in organic chemistry.

The zoology professor, an import from the British Isles, stands out even among the eccentric. He never speaks without arching his eyebrows, creating a faint sense of surprise in everything that transpires. He rushes wherever he goes, his black hair coming along behind. He seems never to notice the rows of us sloping up into the far reaches of the lecture hall. He barks and shouts, as if his energy cannot be contained, certainly not in the softer shapes of the other professors. His is a pre-med course, and we hopefuls have gathered to be entertained and made a little nervous, to be educated. His tests require feats of memory.

In the lab he holds up objects to show us where to cut and what to see. We dissect an ox eye, a frog, a cat. We trace tiny nerves and veins that not long ago carried out their tasks, unaware of the Latin names assigned them. We wear white coats and our hands stink of formaldehyde (and something else besides), our instruments taking us beyond squeamishness into wonder. Mr. Zoo doesn't hesitate to hold back his scorn if we cannot identify the *rectus femoris* and distinguish it from the *vastus medialis*, one lying next to the other or under it, our knowledge of each critical to the grade we will achieve. He snorts and continues down the row of tables, pausing to point and question. He loves to show us what he knows, but also he might just up and whip us, such urgency is brewing in him.

"If you're good," he says, "I'll bring in the brain of a man dead from stroke."

Of course he has favourites, the smartest, most willing to spar. Only one steps into the spotlight, Miss Zitko, who knows she's beautiful: tall, with dark hair, perfect bearing, teeth that somehow please and irritate at the same time. She scores first test after test. He has a way of handing back our papers that makes a point: he starts with the lowest grade and works to the highest. Some poor phys-ed sort usually gets the first paper and the rest of us fall into place, marching up thereafter. I score in the top dozen, but Mr. Zoo scarcely notices me, focused as he is on the drama of the unfolding competition. He knows Miss Zitko is taking his course plus English, French, math, and chem, not a light load, but he's not about to ease up on her.

I study hard. I like Mr. Zoo's unpredictability. His class is big enough to become enjoyable theatre. I enjoy getting lost in the names and weirdness of the flesh world; I like the chance to see under the surface, at first beautiful and repulsive, eventually just facts to be understood and catalogued. I read books and am confused about what to think, since each author is so persuasive. I understand I will not be able to know some truths for certain, but the vein and the nerve on my lab table are unassailable, and I'm happy to stick with them. I'm drawn away from the pointlessness of James Joyce or chemical formulas to put the tip of my scalpel at the very juncture of blood and electrical impulse.

We have no seating order in the classroom, but Miss Zitko is always up front with a number of other young women, none quite up to her standard. I sit in the middle rows, often in the same seat, on the aisle. Mr. Zoo delivers the semifinal tests in his usual manner, starting with the lowest grade. He hands the second-last paper to Miss Zitko, then delivers the last to me, making a point of walking up the aisle to my seat and flourishing it. The air changes for a moment in the class; there seems to be less oxygen, or more carbon dioxide. I see my grade: 97. My face flushes, pride rising. There can be no doubt now. I am first-class, destined to be someone my family never could imagine: a doctor – although the vocation doesn't interest me – but someone, in any case, other than just me. I have the brains and skills to match the best, even beat them. I want to jump out of my seat and whoop, except I feel a little drunk and dizzy.

Miss Zitko is shocked that someone has bettered her, someone she's never even noticed. This experience has jolted her, and I feel embarrassed. Her entourage is eyeing me as well, their faces similarly blank with surprise. I've usurped the Queen of Zoology, and if anyone were to manage such a feat, it should've been one of them, not some collegiate-looking guy in the middle seats.

Mr. Zoo is looking at me, maybe for the first time, and I'm not sure what he's seeing. He sports a look of nearly nasty glee I haven't seen before. He's pleased that someone has topped his best student. He guesses (rightly, as it turns out) that I won't repeat such a feat. Refreshed by the surprise I've brought to his class, he's mostly, I think, glad to see the downfall of Miss Zitko. He turns away from my triumph quickly, to gloat over her reversal, as if she were taking her pre-eminence too much for granted. A new bluster comes to him. He enjoys a fight in his class for the top honour, and this prospect carries him through the term. It helps me as well; when I walk home, I don't think only about the slithering creatures waiting there.

Miss Zitko may be spurred on, too: she wins a major medal when we graduate, two years later, and some small revenge as well. I go up on stage to receive my scroll ahead of her. As I accept it, her triumphs are already being announced to the auditorium by a man in a gown. The audience applauds loudly for her – and because we are nearing the end of the everlasting alphabetical line of undergraduates – and for a foolish moment I think they're clapping for me, intuitively understanding my journey here. But only for a moment. Then she's on stage, and I'm off. She notices not me or the special gleam of relief in the chancellor's eye but only the shiny gold prize.

It occurs to me that Miss Zitko has incorporated little of Mr. Zoo into herself, despite their apparently close – even conspiratorial – connection. She crosses the stage with her prize and her scroll and remains unshakeably herself. No doubt she will become the doctor she already appears to be. Me, I feel far less settled, still looking for the sort of person I will become.

Amid the rustling of gowns, I wonder what it would be like to be Mr. Zoo. It's a hard thing to picture – and it makes me stand quite still in the auditorium – because I cannot see how I will ever take on his assurance and savvy. Yet on one test I triumphed, my little victory safely stowed in that place where I have begun to recognize what I can do when I love a subject enough to go at it calmly and wildly day after day.

❖

Before I fall in love with the woman I will marry, my girlfriend saves me from the terror of being on my own while I wait to find out if I must live forever as someone who has never truly loved. She noticed me in psychology class and perhaps thought I was cute with my big black glasses and pushed-down hair. We make time to listen to each other. She teases me and reads my poetry, and she tells me it's pretty good.

One night she takes me home to her folks for dinner – two tiny Scottish sweeties, the three of them connected in all kinds of code. During the bus ride back across the city, the Russians invade Czechoslovakia. The advertising panels above the bus windows have an extra vividness. Before long I take her home to the farm, where she meets an efficient, garrulous woman and a quiet man, both pleased to see her, curious about this city girl, amused by her ideas of farm life. We take walks in the snow until we long for the city again. We don't yet know, have not yet admitted, that we're not going to stay together much longer. We give each other books. Rod McKuen. *The Collected Irving Layton.*

Meanwhile, she reads my poetry. Poems with months for titles. I do "dark" pretty well, October best of all. I'm still confused by Keats's overload of image and seek something easier, cleaner. I love words that resonate inward. I punch out stanzas on a portable Olivetti, watch as the *h* starts to lose its right leg against the roller. I hunt to see things in a new way, to find the twist that surprises and deepens. Meaning is a shift, a jump that lands neatly in an unexpected place. I write about the seasons without much caring that others have done so, perhaps definitively. On the long bus rides around the city and the longer ones to the farm, I read anthologies with their many ways of showing me the new. I'm involved in the *possibility* that I am a poet.

But. The story of but. I love writing, but what do I know? My girlfriend introduces me to one of her classmates, another young woman, because she thinks we'll like each other. On another campus entirely, one with more students and professors, this new friend offers to show some of my poems to one of her English profs. She describes him: from Dublin, messy black hair falling around his face, prone to compare our university unfavourably with Trinity, where students need only sit on the great steps to hear what must be heard. He's a bit of a ladies' man, and by way of shocking his colonial students he dismisses Hemingway: "*The Sun Also Rises* is the story of a man who lost his balls. Nothing more need be said." I'm apprehensive but feel that if I stay at a distance I'll be buffered against whatever he'll say. I want to know what someone thinks, someone who should know.

I'm a compulsive maker. I enjoy putting together pieces of paper to make little collections, a substitute for publishing. I have a little packet of a dozen poems, my best so far. Most are short, chains of images whose impact derives from the way they turn on themselves. Some of the poems are longer and more descriptive: "On cold days," one begins, "in January / I'd lead the horses out to drink / and they'd come plodding slowly / in a fog of frozen breath . . ."

And so on. What will he think of such a poem? Will he snort and scoff and not believe the feeling behind it (and how will I live with such an appraisal)? Will he think the ending sentimental, melancholic? Or will he maybe hear a voice beyond the subject itself, a voice seeking to catch the sound and the rhythm of a place? It's the end of the academic year, and before long a note arrives from him.

He says I have talent and that if I stick with it I'll be a serious poet someday. I think – I hope – he means it; there's none of the irony and foppishness I've led myself to expect, no implied rejection, only encouragement. An entryway opens that previously I had only wished for. Then, just as suddenly, I'm afraid: what if I work hard and write hard and discover I have nothing to say? What if I commit myself to a future that could never be?

Later, after graduation and a year of teaching, in love with my old girlfriend's friend, the woman who gave my poems to the professor, living with her in a small apartment in another city, I'm hunting and pecking on my Olivetti. I write poem after poem. A few are published in small magazines. Some days, when the work goes poorly, I think of that time when I doubted and a word came from a stranger to tell me the way ahead was clear. Sometimes I suspect even that foolhardy kindness, a polite dispatch to someone unknown. Then I start out again – nothing else to be done – writing, writing, until something comes right.

During one of these urgent spells I stumble on my first real subject. I get a letter from my father, who rarely writes; he talks briefly about his chores, the weather, deer hunting. When I look up from the rain of the city, I see the vastness and snow of the farm, the tiny lines between people. I fumble about, trying to find the right tone. "Father" takes three weeks to write, and when it's done, I'm struck by the emblematic peculiarity of its origin: a man I've never met has freed me to write about my dad. The voluble Irish professor and the melancholic

German farmer warily meet and circle and take up their positions in me.

◈

My father's on a kitchen chair, violin tucked under his chin, bearing down on the instrument with great concentration. Two young men on guitars play chords, following his lead in a foxtrot. Around them neighbours are chatting, plucking up my mother's homemade cookies from card tables with collapsible legs. We've gathered this winter evening to share sweets and tea and pickles and buns and gossip.

Once I looked inside that violin through the *f*-shaped holes and saw old-fashioned writing on a discoloured label. I didn't know how the instrument came into our family but imagined it was valuable and famous, sent to us from music-loving relatives in Germany. I saw an old man packaging it and carefully writing in Gothic script my father's name and address. I saw him take it down the stairs of his house and send it off across the world via train and ship and train again.

After a breather my father begins again. His face sharpens when he plays, displacing the personal ache that every face finally discloses. I see this untroubled face rarely. One photo reveals this man: he is much younger, holding my oldest brother, my sister standing in front of my mother and grandmother. My dad looks at the camera; he's thin, healthy, masculine, urgent, proud of his children, his wife, and his mother, but aware that chores

165

need completing. His clothes are from a different time: pants with pockets that have snaps, shirt rolled up to the forearms. A man in his prime, with the confidence that comes of strength and love and purpose, nothing defeated or settled too soon, the possibilities still awaiting him, one of those possibilities me.

❖

Before I leave the prairies, I get a job teaching in a town so small it has no laundromat, no pool hall. There's one store, one café, one undertaker, one garage. The kids are bused in from farm schools. Once they've gone home, the town gets quiet indeed.

We cover the high school curriculum, Larry, Ralph, Frank, Luke, Ben, and me. No women, which goes without comment in the community (the women teachers are in the elementary school nearby) but not in our staff room. It's Ben's job to make sure we teach the required subjects and manage those no one really understands – i.e., guidance. He's the principal, a good one, I'll say, even though he's so far the only principal I've had. Fresh from a BA and twelve weeks of teacher training, I keep my hair cut short.

I'm close enough to live at home in the fall, back at the farm again after university in the city. The sweetness of being an adult son means I see my parents as characters from a novel and love them the more. I leave every morning at 7:30 in my dad's Chev and drive the back road past Glencairn. I pass fields and pastures, cross railway tracks but rarely see trains. Wind, clouds, dust, sky. The Riding Mountains grow larger as I drive west, their slopes a yellow and orange swath across the bottom of the horizon.

I think about what I'm going to teach this day, remembering who I was in English 11, when they – the forces that, in fact, I have become – kindly reread my failed English final and pushed me on. I recall my former self with chagrin and try to bear his lack of subtlety in mind when I face my students.

Sometimes when I look at them I wonder if I really have left home, if this school is far enough away to count. I don't dwell on it because once the snow comes, the back road is not plowed open. Sometimes only one pair of tracks marks the bottom of the trough made by snowbanks on either side.

The problem now is the one I had in August, when I signed my contract to teach for a year: there's only one place to stay in town. Sam and Ethel offer room and board. They're gentle, good people, but their house consists of a tiny kitchen, a tiny living room, two tiny bedrooms, and a tiny bathroom. I get the smaller bedroom. Naturally I stay away as much as I can. Some weekends, if the weather's decent, I manage to get home. Dad picks me up, or I catch a ride. Often I stay and join with the others in making our own fun in town. Town is what we call it, though it's a village. When the Saturday nights are long, we get together to play whist, and drink.

In the fall, I stay after school to prepare lessons and mark assignments but also to play tennis with Ben. He's made a makeshift court for the kids in the playing field. After they leave, we have a game or two. The racket never quite stops feeling like a club to me, but I enjoy the game because Ben is a good partner. His big Slavic grin helps me understand he doesn't mind beating me and that I shouldn't mind, either. He's short, shorter than his wife, but that doesn't seem a problem. He never wears a tie but always a clean striped dress shirt, even when he's playing tennis. I admire his bark: he can bring students into line when he needs to, but so far I haven't had to send anyone to him. He's made it known that we need to deal with our students ourselves. He's not above laughing at us to avoid bringing his principal's authority to bear. I think of him as a friend, this boss. It's a line we're always aware of except on the court, which makes playing with him fun. There we're just two guys sweating and swearing and leaping and shouting.

When the snow comes, however, volleyball in the gym is our only option. Sometimes students join us, but often it's just two or three of us, late at night, working out the day before going home to bed. None of us except Ben brings much determination to the game. Beyond the winter, which moves slowly, we know the question of future work awaits: do we stay here another year and risk never leaving, or leave and risk not finding a position elsewhere? Through the long tunnel of winter we play cards and drink red wine.

I learned to drink at university by finding that edge on which you locate the best possible hilarity without falling off. Now I'm coming home late, staggering into the tiny house and finding my way to the tiny bedroom. I'm as quiet as possible: I've been brought up to respect the sleep of others. But it's not possible that Sam and Ethel don't hear me. When I get into bed, the bed begins to toss me about. I can't seem to ride it properly. I sit up, think about standing, but I'm tired now, and tired of the wine, wanting it to please pass, to sleep and wake and be myself again.

I settle my head on the pillow. I try once more to will myself into steadiness. Suddenly I'm heaving up the contents of my stomach. A wine-dark mess spreads across my pillow, its revolting acid stink making me empty myself once more. My horror at having puked in my bed – Ethel's bed! – sharpens me considerably.

I try to think what to do next. The stench has begun to fill the room and spill out under the door. I open my window, let in cold air, pull the sheets and pillowcase off the bed, praying I haven't stained the mattress. I wrap the mess together as best I can, hiding at its deepest centre the flotsam of my foolishness and shame.

I have not thought beyond this point. I've only considered my mortification if Ethel and Sam discover what I've done, how low I will sink in their eyes, my certainty that I could not bear to live in their house any longer. A plan emerges in my mind: I will ask my friend to help me. I will go to Ben and wash the pillowcase and sheets in his machine, and return them to the bed later. In the morning, I try to drift through the kitchen with my bundle stowed in a travel bag.

"Breakfast?" Ethel asks.

"No, thank you," I reply. "I'm on my way. And I've made up my bed, so you won't need to bother with it today."

I might as well have sent a telegram: Search the room for evidence. Stop. The worst mess ever seen in this house. Stop.

Does she look and deduce what has happened? I never know, because nothing is said when I return the sheets to the bed. I lie in them that night, wondering what future I will make for myself, but mainly thinking grateful thoughts about Ben, who laughed at me and helped. His machine has cleaned away every last bit of purple stain, and I can pretend I am still decent.

When I depart, in June, it won't be to find another school but to go farther afield – to Toronto, to write, and because the woman I'm smitten with has gone on ahead of me. A few of the guys will try to keep in touch, but I feel I've changed so much – and need to change even more – that I can't stay connected. Even my gratitude for what I learned working with them will come to seem a sign of how immature I was.

❖

In the barn, my father walks past me, cap pushed up on his head, the peak discoloured and stained by sweat. He's his older, more corpulent self now, carrying in his arms a bird, part dull chicken and part vibrant red pheasant. I watch as he tosses the bird into the air where it flutters and comes to rest in a tree. Slowly we back into the barn, pulling the big doors shut. The bird turns to look down at us, but by the time it seeks to rejoin us in the safety of the building, we've closed the doors. It must learn to live on its own.

My father's already sitting on one of the milk stools, indicating that I should pull up another. A ray of light slants through the small dirty window, illuminating bits of suspended chaff. I'm not prepared for his questions.

"Do you remember who the Schnadelbachs are? And the Hoffmans?"

"Kurt and Kate Hoffman are your cousins in Berlin. After the war, you sent them boxes of clothes wrapped in bleached flour sacks with the address written with a grease pencil. They're the children of your father's sister, your Aunt Lina. But who are the Schnadelbachs? I've forgotten."

His mother's family with their last name different from my own – how can I possibly keep track? My dad's mother is a Lambrecht, but she has a brother who's a Schultz, meaning they had different fathers. In my father's face I see that he's not going to explain these connections to me again.

I reach over and run my hand along the smoothness of the manger, where the cows have burnished the wood to a glossy shine with their saggy necks. I find a piece of twine from one of the bales and twirl it around my finger. We liked to take these twines, three of them, and braid them together into a rope we used to tie up the calves.

Once I found a piece of twine hanging from a calf's mouth. When I pulled it, it kept coming and coming, two feet long, three, four. When I finally got it all back from the calf's stomach, the end of it was soft, half-digested, already transformed into something else.

◆

I park in the lot beside the pavilion of the hospital and make my way through hallways and corridors. Sometimes other visitors accompany me up in the elevator but we have little to say, the context the same, the particulars making all the difference. When we step out, nurses smile and offer coffee. They talk about the patient we have come to visit, ever optimistic: "He had a good night" or "His wife was here, and they had a good talk." Murals and paintings cover the walls, the CBC plays music, a sweet dog waits to be petted. Someone has clipped an identity badge to the red bandana around the dog's neck.

I stay a half-hour, an hour, then go back into the rain. I foresee the book I will want to share with my friend, turning towards his looming absence with "Read this, you'll like it" on my lips. Later, at work, someone comes down the hall with news. The way he looks suggests the update will be bad. But the worst doesn't happen then, or the next day, or the next. It's a Tuesday when the call finally comes.

A day later – I can hardly explain it – I'm feeling opened up. This is not the closed-off grief I'm expecting, the kind where the throat doesn't work properly. I feel his presence in my apartment. When the next call arrives, I'm not surprised. My turn has come to stand in for someone who is gone. I'm called upon to speak in his stead.

At the front of the church I see a framed photo of my friend. The photograph steadies me. When the service calls for me to step up, I'm calm. Open faces gaze up at me, wanting to see the man we knew. Women dab their eyes, tilting their heads so the tears will run into tissues. Some men direct their gaze down or blankly ahead. I cannot see the constricted throats, even less the heartache.

On the drive home I imagine the goodbyes ahead: when I enter the office and take down his books, when I hear a certain laugh at the movies and turn to look that way, in dreams of him, in sightings of his beard, his humour, his gait. We're trying to construct the annual teaching timetable for our courses. He doesn't like his schedule – too many night classes, travelling in the dark – and I try to find an earlier version. When I open my filing cabinet, I see the ground, dank and mushy. Then I'm standing with his wife, looking down at a scarecrow once propped up by snow but now lying on the ground, wet and mouldy, a rotting mixture of cloth and straw. In the distance we hear children singing.

Or I see him on the other side of a fence where the grass has grown up to the bottom wire, apparently never cut, flourishing. He's playing with a grey-white ball, dressed in green clothes that match the grass. He kicks the ball in the air and catches it. Then he tosses it over the fence to me. My hands reach up and I feel him, then I throw the ball back to him. When I awake, I wonder if all men return this way, as the grasses and breezes around us.

Then I learn that the father of a young man, an acquaintance, has also died, and that night I dream I'm with him, attending the ceremonies. He's off in another room surrounded by mourners and relatives. We're all packed in. The many people in attendance must be a support – or perhaps they merely postpone the inevitable moment of private grief.

I realize I'm with someone, another man, or more properly a boy just turned man. We stick together when I realize the body is nearby. We make our way towards the room to pay our last respects. I expect an open coffin, the pale corpse inside, flowers around, mourners bending to their hands as they turn away.

I find, instead, that the body has already become part of the real earth of this room, disintegrated, transformed. At his feet – or where his feet would be – tall dry weeds are growing. My companion picks some of these, gripping them by the stems and breaking them. Even more astonishing is the head, which is not really a head but a flat face, an orangeish, plate-sized face without clear features, receding into the earth around it – except for one eye, liquid, vegetable, moving, watching. And I wonder, in my dream, whether death isn't a kind of madness for everyone it touches.

❧

At our house we opened presents on Christmas Eve. Christmas was set aside for the church service and a big meal, so important and traditional that the day couldn't accommodate further festiveness. And besides, we couldn't bear to wait till morning, not when the surprise and sudden uplight of Christmas Eve fell upon us with its twinge of sadness that only the gift of presents could redeem.

We gathered round the tree. When my father took off the wrapping paper and pulled out the glass-encased, ready-to-prop-up graduation picture of me, he began to cry, head down. We were shocked. I didn't know what to say. My brothers stiffened, my sister cried. My mother took the present from his hands and laughed a little. She knew how sentimental our dad could be. I didn't expect him to be moved, and couldn't grasp why he would be: because he was pleased with my success? Because he thought I might not make it? Because I'm the baby of the family? Because life was going by too fast? Because of things more complex and layered than I could ever imagine?

Now a photo in the newspaper sets me wondering. It's of a man about my age, with dark hair and the kind of slope to his belly that means he looks after himself. He's fiddling with his glider. I ask a friend how old she thinks he is. Others gather round. The general agreement is about forty: no grey hair except for a bit in his scraggy beard. I point out that his tight belly is the widest part of him, where his belt circles his girth. He has to be older than forty, though perhaps not by much.

I scan the paper to find his age. And there it is: fifty-seven! Between my father's age and my own. I exclaim aloud that he's in better shape than I am. He's described as trim and neat, and calls himself a Type A personality, someone who likes to win.

I look again and see the aggressiveness more clearly now. That pink shirt – he doesn't think about himself much, is more keen on spotting trouble up ahead and trying to eliminate it before it reaches him. He doesn't spend time musing. He's out the door at dawn, pumping through the rain, getting the job done, having fun with the risk – to the chagrin of the partners in his company. They worry but have long since learned to let go. The thrill of the doing propels him, that kick-ass rush in his muscles even at fifty-seven. He's told them time after time he's not slowing down, not going to retire, can't see the point. He can still prod his body towards the blue ribbon.

His wife left him, but there's another woman now, someone from the office. He's no fool; this second life is different from the first. He accepts her salve on his muscles. But she can't do anything for his knees. They're starting to ache even when he's not on the slopes. Whatever happens, he'll never sit down by the fire with a book.

I mock him but I have no right. I know the value of his take-charge style, a manner I don't have, which compels me to examine those who do. He's the kind of guy you want when the plane goes down and someone has to haul overweight people out of the smoking wreck. He's got advice about shares and funds, and nine out of ten times he's right. He mixes the drinks, changes the tire, pays the kids' tuition. He rails against those who can't just up and do because all the while he feels his heart checking off its days. Were he close to me – as a brother-in-law, say – I would love him for his strength and worry about his pace. In our circle of family and friends I would believe in him, hope for him – and never show my concern, because it would irritate him and be counterproductive. He'd be a man you could never talk to about the death of his father – or maybe you could, briefly, once.

The graduation photo I gave to my father loses its frame and eventually comes back to me. I prop it on my bookcase, contemplate its bent corner and the four white dots where the glass broke and marked the surface of the paper. I stare into those dots. The photo was almost lost, not exactly thrown out but left behind. I became sentimental just in time. Most days I like to see the smooth skin and good teeth of that lad who made my father cry.

That boy didn't grow up to be the man in the pink shirt, though certainly there were days he wanted the punch and drive of such a man. And some days the boy wondered who his ideal perfect father might be. Was he a Type A man? Someone, presumably, never bush-whacked by feelings erupting unexpectedly? Or would he be smart enough, kind enough, to know the father he had was the man he needed all along?

❦

After my parents sold the farm to a neighbour and moved down the road five miles, and before the sale took effect, each of the children claimed something we valued. I chose the upright desk on which I'd learned to write. I strapped it to the top of my car and drove west.

After that final move, I returned to the farm once, finding it less than the paradise I remembered: the grass dry, the barns shabby, the upper storey of the house removed entirely, the garden smaller than I recalled and the wind stronger. I thought of my father, who had lived here almost all his life, and of my grandfather, who had left the Old World never to return. Perhaps I had more in common with that Prussian grandfather than I thought.

At home, I find a place for the upright desk – a secretary desk, we always called it, though I don't know why. In the four small drawers I keep objects of sentimental value. Only one drawer retains the original wood, and it bears the gouging pencil scribbles I absent-mindedly made as a child. The other drawers fell apart, only their front panels with knobs remaining. My father took a tin Coca-Cola sign from a store in town and cut out a shape that he then folded and bent to make a drawer. I admire his ingenuity and resourcefulness still: only four small nails hold the tin to the front panel, the back held by a point where the metal was folded on itself.

Here I keep an object my father called his ort, a piece of wood about two inches long with a golden patina that still carries a slight smell of oil and harvest dust. Embedded in the end of the wood is a thin strong bit of metal, originally the end of a hay-fork tine. My father inserted the metal prong into the wood and used this durable tool to mend the canvas parts of his machines.

Originally the prong was straight, but now it's bent at

the tip (although still strong). Once, when I was bored and curious, I went into the tool shed and tested the strength of the tip against the anvil. I pushed and pushed, expecting it to give at the wood base. Instead it was the tip that bent. I felt my heart beat faster as I carefully buried it among my father's sturdy pliers and rasping files.

❧

When I emerge from a friend's house, where I'm staying, there they are – my two brothers, down on their haunches in the middle of the street, inspecting the back end of the new car. I'm happy to see them, and their bending to the car makes me love them anew. I like their connection to vehicles, the way they engage the material world and wrestle with it. It's a Buick they're admiring now. They turn to me, their faces open, as if conversation about the car has warmed them up. They wonder how I'm doing: last night I drank and danced at the wedding of the son of the brother closer in age to me, the one already retired. In the morning I'd been shaky, but now I settle into the back of the Buick and listen.

The oldest brother has made a life of cars. He knows about the feel of a machine, speaks of driving this Buick on the perimeter highway in the early morning, before seven, on his way to work, going 160 kilometres an hour, 180, no tire noise to speak of, the car solidly on the road. A friend of his drove his Porsche down the same stretch at 210, 250, like landing in a plane, he said, the ground goes by so fast.

My brother's friend is a little crazy, needing to test the car against its manufacturer's guarantee that it could go 310. He drove to Montana where there's no speed limit and found himself travelling, yes, 310 kilometres an hour. The three of us can only imagine such speed, four times our present rate, which is enough to get us anywhere in these soft grey seats, the landscape of the city passing by like a silent movie.

We're grown now, but some part of us wants to put the gas to the floor and feel our backs sink into the leather seats. We want to go so fast that we lift off out of our old lives, the ones where we heckle and love one another no matter what. We want to be some place where we're in control, where we can make things happen by a mere movement of our hands, that shifting of gears that fills us with power and sound.

Each brother is called by his first name but has a second that tells a story. The first-born has my father's name – Alfred – to pay homage to the past, to fatherhood and to all those Germans who lived their fierce and tidy lives in long-ago forests and farms. The second-born's second name – Edward – is borrowed from the Prince of Wales, to show perhaps that we were ready to move towards some future flamboyant with the promise of change.

Both brothers were young when the messages came from the old country: send what you can, woollens please, there's nothing here. My father's cousins were starving and freezing in the post-war years, so we sent boxes of leftover socks, shirts, blankets, all of it wrapped in sturdy brown paper and mailed. Twice a knife came back, bone handle and good German steel that keeps its edge. For as long as I can remember, my father's friends envied the way his blade sliced through the tough hide of a deer.

My brothers were born at home with a German grandmother for a midwife, a matriarch who delivered children any time of day or night within the distance a horse and buggy could reach, harness bells tinkling in announcement. Our grandfather was dead before our mother met our father, swept up by the authorities and interned as an enemy alien in a detention camp in Brandon because one of the neighbours was telling lies, saying Ferdinand had a gun – he did, of course, a rifle, for hunting. He was a gun expert in Germany. He went into the camp with his oldest son and rotted through the winter. His wife's efforts and petitions to obtain his release proved futile. Finally she wrote a letter in German to the prime minister, Robert Borden.

Three weeks later her husband came home. But he was already a ghost, found dead in the fields not long afterwards, passing back to the ground. Ever since we've had inside us, my brothers and me, this need to get away, our mother's unstated ambition for us. And for a while, tucked in a speeding Buick, it feels like we've succeeded.

❧

The party is a simple one. I'm making a salad. I start with the carrots, breaking them into a bowl in my lap; the kitchen is so crowded I can't find room to stand. I need a knife, and I ask if anyone has one. Two neighbour brothers step forward, one pulling a long knife from his pants pocket. It has several options, which he shows me: a main blade – eight inches – several smaller ones, a corkscrew, a screwdriver. He's pleased to demonstrate this knife, but before he's finished, his brother jumps him. Soon they're wrestling on the couch with this open blade tossing around between them. I yell at them to stop because the knife is wedged between their faces. They struggle against each other, each trying to get a headlock, the blade adjacent to both their jugulars. I wonder: where is their father?

I think of those brothers many years later as I'm eating a meal my brother has made for me: new spring potatoes and carrots in a creamy sauce, tasty and fresh. My brother and I and our father are at the kitchen table, talking about the day just ending. I'm savouring the round, small potatoes with each bite, trying not to dribble on the white tablecloth. I've been so busy at work that I haven't been able to cook much, and I'm grateful my brother has made this meal for me. I can taste the new potatoes as if my father has just passed over with the cultivator and pulled them up to the surface; I used to wipe the dirt and thin skin off on my pants and bite into the spud right there.

Father's talking about the cemetery, the need to work on the family graves, weeding and cleaning, raking the gravel, setting the tilted headstones back to upright.

"The graves will be ninety-three years old this year," he says.

My brother turns to him, surprised. "They're not that old."

My father begins calculating on his fingers, but he's unable to figure it out. I wonder: what's the matter with him? Is he thinking of the year 1893, when his parents came here from Prussia? I find a calculator but can't see it clearly in the dark. I reach to turn on the floor lamp but the switch is not working. In the dimness of the dining room I return to the potatoes, relishing how well they've grown under my father's dark soil.

❧

I'm not there when my father turns to the doctor (who has rushed into the room) and tells the flustered young man: "You're too late." An aneurysm kills him the next instant. My father was always a man of few words, often saying nothing when something might usefully be said, and these final words are characteristically direct, a statement without ambiguity. I imagine that the doctor hears the note of criticism as my father's eyes roll up and his soul flies away.

I'm working in Banff, and I've taken the day to hike into the front ranges of the Rockies. The air is clean, the possibility of meeting bears invigorating. I follow the trail with friends. We share treats on the way to a lookout that gives us a view of a wide glaciated valley and rows of mountains disappearing into hazy blue.

As I'm returning to my room, two friends appear. One hands me a pink while-you-were-out slip. On it someone has written: "Call home. Your father died." The letters are carefully formed, a girl's handwriting. I wonder which of the young receptionists took the call. What did she think when she wrote the message? My friends found it tacked to my door. Feeling the need to save me from such efficient bluntness, they prepared me by the way they looked, and by being there when I read the news, which of course instantly overshadowed the manner of its delivery.

I catch the next bus to Calgary, wait at the airport. Tourists surround me with their bags and children, their magazines and paperback novels. Some look tired, others expectant. Is anyone else, I wonder, flying to a father's funeral? Looking at their faces, I see no one here has the expression I feel working its way onto my face. Surely everyone can see what's written there: worry, about my mother and how she's coping. When my father was dying, she said she didn't know "how he was going to get out of this." I wanted to say: "Mum, he's not." Anxiety, that I'll break down at the funeral now that I've crossed this defining line. Sadness, that I long ago resigned myself to not prying from him who he is – who he was – having taken my own step into his kind of detachment, sentimental and judging at the same time.

Another traveller may see relief on my face: that my father's no longer in pain, that I can at last give up the expectation that because he was old, he was close to dying even when he wasn't sick. At least that back-of-mind waiting is over. What that traveller perhaps won't see is the guilt that adorns the relief.

Once before I'd flown home in a hurry, back to the hospital where I'd been born. We had a scare: my father had chronic pain. At first we thought it was his old affliction, stomach ulcer. I grew up with the blue milk of magnesia bottle in the fridge, the pudding my mother cooked for him from stale bread, the list of foods he couldn't eat. But this time the ulcer seemed worse, something we couldn't talk about, the doctor unwilling to say much either. My father was wrapped in a hospital gown, collapsed on the pillows, his grey hair plastered to his head, his hand near the swivelling food tray with its untouched meal.

I sat by his bed, wanting to say something, hoping what I was feeling would be communicated. I held the railing and looked at him. I touched him on the hand and listened as others spoke of him as if he weren't here. This was the time for me to speak, but what would I say that hadn't been said? There seemed no point in saying I loved him, having flown halfway across the country – I was there, wasn't I? The male flaw: surely my presence spoke more clearly than any trite expression I might manage.

We knew Dad was dying when he started to go blind. Taking off his glasses, he'd grip them by the corners of the frames, correctly, not yanking them off by one arm, which is my usual way. He'd rub his eyes, watery but still hard to meet, or meet for long. He said his glasses were letting him down. He said they couldn't stop his eyes from rolling up. He blamed the glasses, wanting to spare us what he knew.

His glasses always fogged up when he came into the house in winter. He'd be working outside in the dim afternoon cold, and when he stepped inside, the lugs pulled down over his ears, his big mitts on, his glasses would abruptly go white, opaque. He'd become a spaceman for a moment, from another world. Then he'd stomp the snow off his boots.

When he took off his glasses, he'd look around as if surprised to see he'd landed here, with this family. His naked face seemed to be asking questions. Then he'd turn to the immediate task: clearing the lenses so he could see again inside the warm kitchen, quiet but for the sound of potatoes boiling on the wood stove.

Now, in the small house, family members greet one another in teary embrace, aware of the absence in the kitchen. One of my brothers sits outside with his memories, away from the talking. I ask how he is, and he says he just wants the next two days to be over. We find places to sleep. Next day we will have to get rid of my father's shoes. We can't bear the way they curl up, the way my mother looks at them with such longing and bewilderment.

Most arrangements have already been made – the hospital, the church, the pallbearers, the plot, the hymns, the undertaker. Someone asks who's been engaged to dig the grave. The Ladies' Aid will offer tea and sandwiches afterwards in the basement of the church. Meanwhile, neighbouring women stop briefly with casseroles. When the men come by, they talk to my older brothers but don't enter the house. I hear them through the screen door; I'm sitting in my father's chair, reading and remembering. They talk about the weather, the sadness, the weather, the sadness.

One task remains before the funeral: travel to the

nearby village, where the undertaker lives and where, as a family, we will view my father's body. As we walk past the lilacs that have already bloomed it's hard to imagine that behind the weathered boards of this small out-building is a coffin, flowers, a few chairs, a body. I don't like this ritual, though I understand the need to visit one last time.

The last time I saw him he was in hospital; what remains of him is his high forehead, his big ears, his hands crossed on his chest, his good grey suit and tie. My brothers can't bear more than a look. My mother lingers. My sister cries and stays close to my mother, clinging. Both touch him, adjust his tie, pat his lapels; they see beyond the stiffness and pallor, the closed eyes, the mouth wired shut.

"Alfred will be remembered by his wife, Teenie, for being such a loving husband. She could never rouse an angry word out of him, he was just too much of a caring person. By his children, for the loving attention he gave them. By his friends and neighbours for his openness, his honesty, and his willingness to lend a hand whenever needed."

Weeks later, remembering the ceremony, I become suddenly, vividly mindful of my father's traits in me, perhaps the very ones he received from his father. I'm aware, as I never was during his lifetime, that I've been forged by contact – of flesh, of soul – with this man, aware that he's the person I've rubbed against, to become.

And now, everywhere I look, I see not just men but sons, and not just sons but the fathers in them.

The text in this book is set in Bembo, a typeface produced by Stanley Morison of Monotype in 1929. Bembo is based on a roman typeface cut by Francesco Griffo in 1495; the companion italic is based on a font designed by Giovanni Tagliente in the 1520s.


Book design by Blaine Herrmann